Hereof, Thereof, and Everywhereof

A Contrarian Guide to Legal Drafting

Howard Darmstadter

Section of Business Law
American Bar Association

Defending Liberty
Pursuing Justice

The materials contained herein represent the opinions of the author and should not be construed to be the action of the American Bar Association or the Section of Business Law unless adopted pursuant to the bylaws of the Association.

Nothing contained in this book is to be considered as the rendering of legal advice for specific cases, and readers are responsible for obtaining such advice from their own legal counsel. This book is intended for educational and informational purposes only.

Much of the material in this book originally appeared as a series of columns in *Business Law Today,* the official magazine of the American Bar Association's Section of Business Law.

Library of Congress Cataloging-in-Publication Data

Darmstadter, Howard.
   Hereof, thereof, and everywhereof : a contrarian guide to legal
Drafting / by Howard Darmstadter.
      p. cm.
Includes index.
   ISBN 1-59031-077-2 (paperback)
1.   Legal composition. 2. Law—United States—Humor. I. Title.
KF250 .D37 2002
808'.06634—dc21
   2002004238

Cover design by Shepherd Incorporated.

Discounts are available for books ordered in bulk. Special consideration is given to state and local bars, CLE programs, and other bar-related organizations. Inquire at Book Publishing, American Bar Association, 750 N. Lake Shore Drive, Chicago, Illinois 60611.

06 05 04 03 02   5 4 3 2

To the memory of my father
Herbert Joseph Darmstadter
1897–1963

TABLE OF CONTENTS

PREFACE

This book could get you into a lot of trouble. It's about legal drafting—surely one of life's drier subjects—but its approach and recommendations are decidedly nonstandard. Junior associates are warned!

Lawyers seldom welcome innovations in document design and language for understandable reasons. Law is complicated. No one knows more than a fraction of the legal principles he might someday need, and practitioners rarely have the time for academic meditation. In the turmoil that surrounds most transactions, lawyers are reluctant to dispense with standard phraseology no matter how obscure. Incomprehensible matters are simply assumed to be important. Anyone who questions a provision may be told, in all sincerity, that the provision and its language are time- or court-tested. The process of drafting a legal document does not encourage tinkering.

The process of legal drafting typically begins with an associate dragging examples out of the firm's form file and changing the names, dates and description of the transaction. Particular provisions are then modified to suit the singularities of the business deal. When the deal is done, the new document is added to the form file, ready for the next associate.

One might defend the process as accretional: With each redrafting, the document is thought to attain a higher degree of legal sophistication. On this view, the numerous twists and turns of the document are seen as embodiments of subtle legal ingenuity.

Maybe. But the examples the associate drags from the form file don't explain their provisions, and the associate is unlikely to know the factual or legal contingencies that motivated them. Someone working on the transaction may remember the genesis of a recently drafted provision. The reasons for other provisions may have been learned in law school. Regardless, much of the document will be obscure to everyone. In a profession that turns entire forests into legal documents, there is little written that explains their standard provisions.

Much that is strange and obscure in legal documents reflects a legal, technological and cultural milieu that is no longer extant. My concern in this book is to clear the ground of obsolete legal conventions and to advance a style of drafting better suited to current conditions, especially to some recent technological innovations.

Don't worry; the technological changes I refer to are already thoroughly integrated into everyday legal practice—word processors, laser printers, fax machines and photocopiers. We can exploit these familiar technologies to produce documents that are less painful for our readers.

This book offers a number of tips that are easy to implement and likely to improve most legal documents. It is not, however, a guide to good writing. My concerns are almost exclusively with the problems of *legal* documents. Legal writers have much to gain from books on writing generally, but such a book is beyond my range.

Much of this book is devoted to explaining the reason for the suggestions I make. It's not a particularly learned book, however, because I lack the facilities and the temperament for sustained historical research. Rather, it is a form of speculative anthropology. I've been ostensibly practicing business law for over two decades; however, as I tell my friends, I've really just been doing fieldwork. I live my working days amidst a strange tribe of scriveners whose manners I struggle to understand. I participate in the natives' rituals and then guess as to how these antics came to be. I flatter myself that I may, in these pages, have explained some small behaviors.

I've been writing a column, Legal-Ease, for *Business Law Today,* the magazine of the American Bar Association's Section of Business Law, since 1993. Much of the material in these pages first appeared in *Business Law Today* in a somewhat different form.

INTRODUCTION:
YOUR AUDIENCE

When I was in law school, many of my fellow-students shunned the practice of business law. They weren't in law, they said, to make money; they were in law to "help people."

I have no doubt that they were sincere, and I imagine that most of them did end up helping people. But so did I. The people I help have titles like "assistant treasurer," but they're people nonetheless, and, God knows, they have problems. They value my help, and I value their confidence in me.

These people are my audience. They are sophisticated people, but they are not lawyers. They want legal advice and "legal" documents, but their concerns are not primarily legal. I try to write documents that address their concerns.

To say my audience is not composed of lawyers is not to say that they are ignorant of legal concepts. My audience knows what a security interest is, and most of them know that security interests must be perfected. Joint and several liability is a familiar concept to them, as is a voidable preference.

I'm lucky. I know most of the initial audience for my documents by their first names. Several of them will read the document and ask for clarifications before the document goes to the strangers on the other side (although I'm getting to know lots of people on the other side too). I think I know what my audience wants.

Knowing your audience is the first step to good legal drafting. If your documents are going to help your audience with their problems, you have to understand their problems, hopefully in the way they understand them.

Sometimes you will not know your audience. I've recently been involved in drafting securities prospectuses. I'm not sure who reads prospectuses and why, so I write for a hypothetical investor.

My approach to legal drafting has a good deal in common with the "plain language" school. I like plain talk. However, I draft my agreements (and even most of my prospectuses) for sophisticated businesspeople, not consumers. I use legal concepts that are familiar to my audience, although not to most laymen. I also feel free to use trade jargon without explanation. It's appropriate when I'm drafting for my audience.

LEGAL DRAFTING GENERALLY

WORDS

Few aspects of legal writing excite as much scorn from the public, or seem to be so ripe for reformation, as the lawyer's vocabulary. But here, I am afraid, I must disappoint. I have not conducted any elaborate survey of legal language, and I have no wish to retail what others have done.[1] What follows instead is a limited grab-bag of suggestions for reforming some of those unwieldy locutions that, in my own practice, have most frequently or forcibly imposed themselves upon me, followed by some reflections on grammar and nomenclature.

THE LEGAL CLUMSIES

Legal documents require a certain amount of legal language, but the document should still be as close to colloquial English as practicable. Writing colloquial English is not easy. If I were better at it, I'd be writing novels rather than documents. So what follows are just a few useful suggestions.

Use articles. Lawyers tend to use *any* instead of *a* and *such* instead of *the,* as in *Any Bank may . . . if such Bank . . . .* This would read better as *A Bank may . . . if the Bank . . . .*

Use *if.* The cumbersome *In the event that . . .* can usually be replaced by *If . . . .*

Use prepositions. Locutions such as *in the case of* and *with respect to* can often be replaced by a preposition. For example, *In the case of Euro-loans . . .* becomes *For Euro-loans . . . .*

---

1. A book with useful observations on legal vocabulary is DAVID MELLINKOFF, LEGAL WRITING: SENSE AND NONSENSE (1982).

3

Use 's for possessives. *Company's officers* is usually better than *officers of the company,* and *the company and its officers* is always better than *the company and the officers thereof.*

Use present tense. Lawyers tend to use *shall* for imperatives, e.g., *the Borrower shall notify . . . ,* and *may* for permissive acts. This is acceptable, but lawyers also use *shall* and *may* in other contexts where the results are less desirable. For example, *If the Borrower shall be unable to . . .* is awkward. *If the Borrower is unable to . . .* does nicely.

Avoid the extraneous *certain*. My ancient Webster's Collegiate Dictionary gives one meaning of *certain* as "one or more specific things or persons not further described." If you don't know what it is that distinguishes the *certain* things or persons, or if distinguishing them isn't important for present purposes, you can usually drop *certain* or replace it with *some,* as in *and* ~~certain~~ *other costs described below* and *the issuer may sell* ~~certain~~ **some** *certificates of a series by means of this prospectus.*

Avoid unnecessary time references. Documents can become cluttered with unnecessary time references such as *at any time, from time to time, past, present or future,* and so forth. Because everything that happens, happens in time, much of this verbiage is unnecessary. Change *at the time of* to *when* and *during the period of* to *while.*

Avoid unnecessary rights and obligations language in agreements. Most agreements begin with something like *the parties agree that,* which qualifies everything that follows. After such an introduction, you don't need to say that Acme Corp. *shall be obligated [or required] to, agrees that it shall* or *has the right [or power] to.* Replace the first two with *Acme Corp. shall [or will]* and the last with *Acme Corp. may.*

Use *including* without *but not limited to* or *without limitation.* If you're not comfortable with using *included* by itself, you can add a paragraph to the "usages" section to explain that *including* means *including, but not limited to.*[2]

---

2. The usages section is described in "Untangling the Legal Sentence—Sentences That Do Too Much" at 20.

Avoid the extraneous *amount.* Because payments (and many other things) come prepackaged in amounts, *increase the payment* rather than *increase the amount of the payment* says it all.

Avoid extraneous occurrences and effects. In place of *Any occurrence of interest losses will have the effect of reducing . . . ,* try *Interest losses will reduce . . .* instead. Similarly, it is better to use *by* rather than *on or before* or *not later than,* and *as* rather than *in the capacity of.* Simple single words rather than ornate phrases.

HEREOF, THEREOF, AND EVERYWHEREOF

A few legal terms are so ubiquitous that they deserve special treatment. I refer, of course, to terms beginning with *here, there* or *where* combined with *of, in, by, under, before* or *after.* They're a brutish lot; their distance from common speech makes them prime candidates for the chop, and they are usually easily dispensed with.

Thereof. *Thereof,* as in "the company and the officers thereof," is usually easily replaced by *its,* as in "the company and its officers."

Hereof. *Hereof,* as in "section 2 hereof," can simply be dropped; the agreement's "usages" section should explain that, unless otherwise stated, section references are to sections of the document. Hereof, as in "the enforceability hereof," however, would be better written "the enforceability *of this agreement.*" I don't normally approve of replacing one word with three, but I'll make an exception where the word replaced is both archaic and vague.

Yes, vague. Words like *hereof* and *thereof,* which smack so of legal precision, are, in fact, quite imprecise.[3] How could it be otherwise? Would you normally think that *here, there* or *where* themselves are models of precise reference? In "the enforceability hereof," is the reference to the sentence in which the phrase occurs the paragraph, the section or the entire document? Many documents provide that *here,* as in *hereof* and *hereby,* refers to the entire document, but what cure is there for the ambiguity in "the enforceability *thereof*"?

---

3. I'm not the first to make this point. *See, e.g.,* MELLINKOFF, *supra* note 1, at 1–12.

Hereinafter. *Hereinafter* is mainly encountered in definitions, as in "Acme Corp. (hereinafter, the *Borrower*)." Nowadays almost everyone appreciates that a term in parentheses and in quotation marks or italics is a definition. *Hereinafter* may therefore be dispensed with. (*Hereafter* is sometime used in place of *hereinafter. Hereafter* is found in ordinary speech, but as a noun denoting the undiscovered country from whose bourne, etc. One might conceivably use it in drafting a will, but not in a business law document.) The other uses of *hereinafter* and its equally bloated sibling, *hereinbefore,* can usually be replaced by the less rotund *below* and *above.*

Hereunder. *Hereunder* can be replaced with "under this agreement (section, paragraph, etc.)."

Hereby. A particular favorite. You can usually just leave it out, as in *Acme Corp. [hereby] agrees* . . . . There may be circumstances where *hereby* might clarify that the subject is taking an action rather than merely describing an action taken elsewhere, although I can't say I have ever seen such an instance. If you think you've got one, use "Acme Corp., by this instrument [paragraph, etc.] agrees that . . . ." If you find yourself doing this more than once a year, you're probably overdoing it.

Thereafter. *Thereafter* can usually be replaced by *afterwards,* although both are a bit awkward. Unlike the other words in this list, my prejudice against *thereafter* does not run deep.

Whereby. *Whereby,* as in "section 33 of the Inebriation Act, whereby the Commission is authorized . . ." may be better written as "section 33 of the Inebriation Act authorizes the Commission . . ." or "the Commission is authorized by section 33 of the Inebriation Act . . . ," depending on what you want to stress.

I don't object to legal terminology where it's necessary to express a legal concept that has no compact equivalent in nonlegal speech. That can't be said of *hereof, thereof* and their ilk. One of the unfortunate effects of their use is that they can be substituted for legal reasoning. I vividly remember that, when I was a kid lawyer, liberally sprinkling hereofs and thereofs on a document was enough to convince me that I was indeed a hotshot drafter.

WORDS AND NUMBERS

In 1986, a legal secretary typed "$92,885.00" in a ship mortgage when he should have typed "$92,885,000.00." When the lender, Prudential Insurance, went to foreclose, it nearly came up three orders of magnitude short. Luckily for Prudential, the courts eventually saved all but about $11 million of its bacon.[4]

Some lawyers take *Prudential*'s lesson to be that caution dictates using both words and numerals in giving dollar amounts. I fail to see the logic. True, if our hapless secretary had typed "ninety-two million eight hundred eighty five thousand dollars and no cents ($92,885.00)," Prudential might have been better off. Article 3 of the UCC (which didn't govern in *Prudential*) states that "words prevail over numbers."[5] Suppose, however, that our secretary typed "ninety two thousand eight hundred and eighty five dollars ($92,885,000.00)"? Prudential might then have wished it had just typed the numerals. Clearly, the best practice is to type whichever—words or numerals—is least likely to result in mistakes.

I've conducted no empirical research (*What do you mean, "empirical research"? We're lawyers!*), but it seems easier to read numerals than words. Admittedly, events have proved that it's possible to misread "$92,885.00" as ninety-two million, etc., dollars. But it's easier to read "$187,516,714" than "one hundred eighty seven million five hundred sixteen thousand seven hundred fourteen dollars." (The consistent spelling out of numbers is one of those devices that makes New York's statutes so delightful to read.)

Although numerals are generally easier to read, there is an exception: It's easy to misread a string of identical numerals, such as the string of zeros in *Prudential*. Where the identical numerals are zeros, however, there is an easy solution: Write numbers as numerals, but use words in place of final triplets of zeros. Thus, "$187,516,714," but "$10.2 million" rather than $10,200,000.

---

4. *Prudential Ins. Co. of America v. SS American Lancer,* 870 F.2d 867 (2d Cir. 1989). The hairbreadth escape of the law firm that gave the opinion on the mortgage's enforceability is recounted in 80 N.Y.2d 377 (1992).

5. U.C.C. § 3-114 (1990).

(I still write "$162,000," however, because "$162 thousand" looks a bit odd.)

Incidentally, Prudential was probably helped to its $11 million loss (now wasn't that number easy to read?) by some pedantic soul's insistence on specifying the amount to the penny even when there weren't any pennies. It's easy to read "$92,885.00" as "$92,885,000."

WE AND YOU, WILL AND SHALL

Lawyers who would no more leave out a plump bit of boilerplate from an agreement than go to work without their socks may still allow themselves to do without these clauses in a letter agreement. Letter agreements also lend themselves to two particular sorts of informality: Referring to the parties as *we* and *you* and replacing *shall* with *will*.

Using *we* and *you* is championed by the plain language school of drafting, especially for consumer contracts. In a printed consumer contract, there can be no doubt that *you* refers to the consumer reading the contract. The reader of a letter agreement, however, can easily lose her bearings. Deep in the interior of a 10-page letter agreement, "we" may be no more helpful a reference than "the party of the first part."

Still, referring to the parties as *we* and *you,* if it can be done without confusion, produces less-stilted text. You might therefore consider beginning your letter agreement with:

> This letter will confirm the agreement between Midas Bank, N.A. ("we" or "Bank") and Micawber Manufacturing Company ("you" or "Micawber").

This way you can use *we* and *you* when there is no possibility of confusion and *Micawber* and *Bank* elsewhere. For example, a provision as to when "we may charge your account" is unlikely to confuse Bank or Micawber.

Judiciously referring to the parties as *we* and *you* may make a document flow a little easier. You don't have to take my word for it. The SEC's position is that:

. . . another effective tool for producing plain English documents is to use personal pronouns. Personal pronouns immediately engage your readers' attention. A familiar writing style where "we" or "I" refers to management or the company, and "you" refers to the investor, involves your reader and increases comprehension.[6]

You got a problem with *we*? See my regulator.

How about using *will* rather than *shall*? Surprisingly, the will versus shall question is linked to the decision to use *we* and *you*.

The Oxford English Dictionary and Fowler's *Modern English Usage* are of the view that, in British English, *shall* in the second and third person (you, he, she, it and they) expresses the speaker's determination or insistence, whereas *will* expresses mere futurity. In the first person (I, we), it's the reverse, with *shall* expressing the simple future and *will* indicating determination. Fowler illustrates the distinction with a nifty quote from P.G. Wodehouse:

> "I *will* follow you to the ends of the earth," replied Susan, passionately. "It will not be necessary," said George. "I am only going to the coal-cellar. I shall spend the next half-hour or so there."[7]

Things get a bit more complicated (or simpler?) in the colonies. Fowler notes that:

> . . . in the standard English of countries outside England, the absence of *shall* and the omnipresence of '*ll* and *will* are very marked, *e.g.,* United States.[8]

Even in England, some argue that the use of *shall* in the first person to indicate mere futurity is old-fashioned and widely ignored.

---

6. Release 33-7380.
7. FOWLER, A DICTIONARY OF MODERN ENGLISH USAGE 707 (Rev. 3d ed. 1996).
8. *Id.*

Neither the OED nor Fowler comments on the legal import of shall versus will. It's understandable, however, that a lawyer might use the more determined "you shall" to impress upon the parties that a legal obligation is involved, but it's hardly necessary. Micawber isn't legally bound to do something because the document says "Micawber shall" rather than "Micawber will." Micawber is bound because the document says that "the parties agree that" Micawber shall or will perform its humble tasks.

If you use *you will* in a letter agreement, do you complement it with *we shall* or *we will*? Fowler and the OED say it should be *we shall*; others regard *we shall* as out of line with modern trends in American-as-she-is-spoke.

This brings us to one of life's larger questions: To what extent should we feel constrained to follow the OED, Fowler or any other authority on style or grammar? For some, *shall* conveys a sense of legal obligation whether it's *we shall* or *you shall*. Could it be that the OED's rules for *shall/will* are a bit of pure proscription?

For lawyers, the answer is easy. We thrive on proscriptions, rules and authorities. A LEXIS search I conducted a few years ago disclosed 445 citations to the OED and 23 citations to Fowler in the federal courts since 1944. If you try to convince a court that *we shall* is more emphatic than *we will,* you are likely to lose.

SPLITTING INFINITIVES, WHICH VERSUS THAT

What about two other stylistic bugaboos: splitting infinitives and conflating *which* and *that*?

On splitting infinitives, Fowler is tolerant: Split infinitives are undesirable in themselves but are preferable to real ambiguity or patent artificiality. Thus, Fowler might applaud "to boldly go where no man has gone before" for being less awkward than "boldly to go" and less wimpy than "to go boldly."

Fowler's distinction between "which" and "that," a distinction with which I lacked acquaintance for my first 40 years, is another matter. Fowler states that:

. . . if writers would agreed to regard *that* as the defining relative pronoun, and *which* as the non-defining, there would be much gain both in lucidity and ease.[9]

Thus, "the play *that* I saw yesterday," but "Hamlet, *which* [not that] I saw yesterday."
Fowler adds, however, that:

Some there are who follow this principle now; but it would be idle to pretend that it is the practice either of most or of the best writers.[10]

Fowler is right that many famous writers (Jane Austen and P.G. Wodehouse being the latest I have noticed) are not scrupulous about the distinction, if they recognize it at all. Should we observe it?

I have come to recognize the distinction in my own and other's writings so that "the play which I saw yesterday" leaves a mental tremor. I never correct it in other people's writing—life is short—but I don't feel comfortable with it. So the ultimate reason (for me) to follow Fowler's suggestion as well as other grammatical and stylistic rules is to avoid those dissonances that (not which) might distract my reader. Following the rules is less likely to be noted than breaking them.

This is a logic that makes me uneasy, however. The penchant to follow grammatical and stylistic rules—to write and speak in a particular way—is a function of class and education. Why condemn people who haven't our advantages? And if it's all right for them, why isn't it all right for us?

The quick, and probably correct, answer is that written communication requires some conformity to the reader's expectations. Most of my readers are lawyers, many of whom may notice deviations from the sanctioned uses of *shall* and *will, which* and *that.* No sense being thought a booby, so I tend to obey the

9. *Id.*
10. *Id.*

grammatical and stylistic conventions I know about, although I may break them if I think it will produce a useful effect.

How much more widely should this lesson apply? Not too widely, I hope. It has been years since I've fastened my collar button and tightened my tie, and I've taken to wearing crepe-soled shoes. These mild departures from the conventions of legal dress were adopted for comfort, not to communicate my *persona*. It's possible, however, that those who deal with me might take my appearance as an indication that I am less competent than the carefully buffed corporate lawyers they are used to.

On the other hand, because I am occasionally unconventional in legal matters, my appearance may serve as a warning that things may proceed differently than with your regulation legal eagle. In any case, being an in-house lawyer, I don't have to worry about my clients' first impressions. When I was in a law firm, I dressed differently.

The lesson? People pick up what cues they can from language just as they do from dress. If you're striving for a particular effect, you may loosen your tie or split an infinitive, but you want to be in control of your effects. An unappreciated grammatical or stylistic gaffe, like an unnoticed gravy stain on your tie, may undo the effect you want.

One effect that you may try to control is the extent to which a document calls for extensive lawyering. Letter agreements may be less formal than other agreements because the drafter wants to reach a quick conclusion (a motive some lawyers find reprehensible). Referring to the parties as *we* and *you* may further the drafter's goal. So may using the informal American "we will," or even "we'll," rather than the stiffly correct British "we shall." On other occasions, a drafter may opt for the full formal treatment. There are a lot of moves to this game.

NAMING AND MIS-NAMING

A long time ago when my mother was just out of high school, she briefly worked as a legal secretary. What she remembers from the experience is how oddly the lawyers wrote. "The said party of the first part was always doing something or other with the said party of the second part," she recounted. The language seemed bizarre to her then, and it seems bizarre to us now.

The main problem with the-party-of-the-first-part terminology is not that it's ornate, but that it's confusing. It's easy to get the parties reversed because there's no logic behind the numbering system. Contrast the arbitrary numbering of the parties with the numbering system for the bases in baseball, which carries with it the notions of progression (from first to second to third) and accomplishment (home). Consider further how the numbering system for streets and avenues makes most of Manhattan so easy to navigate—although, in the Lobachevskian (or is it Riemannian?) world of Greenwich Village, tenth and fourth streets are allowed to intersect.

Lawyers today don't use any naming system as perversely confusing as the one that so tickled my Mom's funnybone. But there are still plenty of legal terminological tricks that leave clients—and sometimes their lawyers—befuddled. For example, lawyers like to distinguish between bleep*ors* and bleep*ees*. The bleep*or* is the one who bleeps, and the bleep*ee* the one who is bleeped. That's not a wonderful terminological scheme even if you know what bleep you're talking about, as in grantor/grantee or indemnitor/indemnitee. In cases such as mortgagor/mortgagee or lessor/lessee, where there's no obvious indication as to who is bleeping whom, the terminological convention has to be committed to memory. Lawyers who work in the area become comfortable with the distinctions, but that's not a good argument for an awkward nomenclature.

I'm not sure I know a universal solution to the bleepor/bleepee disease. There are, however, excellent solutions for particular contexts. For example, if the lease is of real property, landlord/tenant has all the clarity that lessee/lessor (*oops!* lessor/lessee) lacks.

When I said I wasn't sure I knew a general solution to the bleepor/bleepee terminology, I wasn't just being modest. There is an obvious solution, but I'm not sure how I feel about it. We could call every actor (and actee) by its proper name. We wouldn't refer to xyz Bank as "mortgagee" but as . . . xyz Bank! What could be simpler?

I suspect that one reason lawyers refer to parties by legal category rather than proper name is a hangover from the days when lawyers used more preprinted forms. If you're not stuck with a preprinted form, then replacing 400 occurrences of "mortgagee" by 400 occurrences of "xyz Bank" in a word-processed document is the work of moments. So why not do it?

One situation where legal category terminology ("mortgagee" or "lender") might be preferable to proper name terminology (xyz Bank) is where several sister companies are involved, all with confusingly similar names. In such a case, identifying some of the players by legal categories ("borrower" or "guarantor") can make things less confusing. There are also agreement forms that are so familiar and standardized that lawyers and clients feel comfortable with the traditional terminology. In general, however, using proper name terminology can often make documents less confusing.

So far I've been talking mainly about terminology that is confusing, but terminology can also be *misleading* or simply *unenlightening*. Confusing terminology brings you to a turning and lets you take the wrong road. Misleading terminology, in contrast, gives you the wrong directions. Unenlightening terminology provides no help, but at least lets you know it.

For example, in most syndicated lending arrangements, the bank lenders are represented by an agent bank that is empowered to act upon the request of a specified percentage of the lenders. This percentage of lenders is sometimes referred to as the *majority lenders*. This is a useful terminology *if* the required percentage is in fact 51%. I have seen *majority lenders* used, however, where the required percentage is 67%. That's misleading. I have also seen both percentages referred to as the *required lenders*. That's unenlightening.

Here the solution seems obvious: Use *majority lenders* if the percentage is 51%, *two-thirds of the lenders* if the percentage is 67%, and so forth.

In many agreements, a company must make representations about those of its subsidiaries above a certain size. The terminology often used for those subsidiaries is *material subsidiaries*. This is bad terminology for at least two reasons.

First, the terminology misapplies the word *material*. Lawyers scatter *materials* freely through their documents, although they often find themselves fumbling when the client asks "How much is material?" Actually, *material* has a simple definition: Something is material if it matters. (The U.S. Supreme Court has a famous longer formulation to the same effect.[11]) References to materiality are designed to compensate for the documentational seizures that often result from too-precise drafting. "Material" signals us: *Apply Common Sense Here!*

It is therefore self-defeating to define *material*—a word whose virtue is its eschewal of a false precision—in terms of a numerical test based on balance sheet concepts.

The second objection is that the "material subsidiary" locution isn't informative. If we want to characterize the relevant subsidiaries as those that, for example, have more than 1% of consolidated total assets or consolidated net worth, we can call them *one percent subsidiaries*. That terminology doesn't answer all questions (One percent of what?), but it's a step in the right direction.

It is common for loan agreements to have covenants against the borrower's issuing certain types of guaranties or incurring certain types of debt. In order to prevent the borrower from getting around the covenant, "guaranty" and "debt" are often defined in ways that sweep in arrangements that may have the economic effect of, but are not, guaranties or debt. For example, a borrower's "guaranty" of a subsidiary's debt might be defined to include an arrangement where the borrower pledges assets to secure its own debt and then advances the proceeds to the subsidiary.

There's good reason for a covenant to sweep in this type of quasi-guaranty, but the arrangement isn't a guaranty and

---

11. "An omitted fact is material if there is a substantial likelihood that a reasonable shareholder would consider it important in deciding how to vote. . . . Put another way, there must be a substantial likelihood that the disclosure of the omitted fact would have been viewed by the reasonable investor as having significantly altered the 'total mix' of information available." *TSC Indus., Inc. v. Northway,* 426 U.S. 438, 449 (1976).

shouldn't be called one. What should it be called? How about a *quasi-guaranty*? The covenant can then be phrased in terms of guaranties and quasi-guaranties.

Much the same thing happens with lawyers' definitions of "debt." For example, it is common to see debt of others guaranteed by the borrower defined as "debt" of the borrower. Again, there are good reasons for having covenants against such off-balance-sheet debt, but it would be preferable if the complications went into the covenant rather than into distorting the meaning of a useful and once well understood term.

What strikes me about all of the above examples is how easy it is to devise a more appropriate terminology. All that was needed was the conviction that things should be called what they are and not what they aren't.

> "The question is," said Alice, "whether you *can* make words mean so many different things."
>
> "The question is," said Humpty Dumpty, "which is to be master—that's all."
>
> Alice was too much puzzled to say anything; so after a minute Humpty Dumpty began again. "They've a temper, some of them—particularly verbs: they're the proudest—adjectives you can do anything with, but not verbs—however, *I* can manage the whole lot of them! Impenetrability! That's what *I* say!"[12]

---

12. Lewis Carroll, Through the Looking-Glass and What Alice Found There ch. VI (1871).

UNTANGLING THE LEGAL SENTENCE

Lawyers' sentences are more tangled than almost anybody else's sentences. This is due in part to the complexity of the logic:

> Archie will pay Betty $10 on Sunday, if it rains, $20 if it snows, and $50 if there's a hurricane, unless the Dodgers win the World Series, in which case . . .

and partly to the difficulty of describing the subject matter:

> Jughead agrees to wash all the exterior parts of Archie's car, including the tires but not including the underside of the car, and to clean the passenger compartment, including vacuuming the upholstery and washing the interior glass, instrument panel and the steering wheel and other controls, but not the pedals or anything under the instrument panel or in the glove compartment, except that . . .

But the complexity of the logic and the subject matter merely presents a special lawyer's problem: How do you say complicated things in a way that can be easily understood? In this chapter, I present some tools for cutting through the sentential tangle.

Sentences That Run Too Long

Long-windedness is one of the lawyer's least lovable traits. "Ask a lawyer the time of day and he'll tell you how to build a watch," goes the old refrain.

17

In documents, long-windedness affects both the document as a whole and its component sentences. Consider the following 286-word sentence—a subordination provision inserted in a promissory note—produced by a prominent law firm (I've added six bracketed numbers for reference purposes).

> Upon (i) any payment being required to be made by the Obligor under the Junior Indebtedness upon any declaration of acceleration of the principal amount thereof or (ii) any payment or distribution of assets of the Obligor of any kind or character, whether in cash, property or securities, to creditors upon any dissolution or winding up or total or partial liquidation or reorganization of the Obligor, whether voluntary or involuntary or in bankruptcy, insolvency, receivership or other proceedings, [1] all principal, premium, if any, and interest due or to become due upon all the Superior Indebtedness of the Obligor shall first be paid in full, or payment thereof provided for in money, before any payment is made under Junior Indebtedness; [2] and upon any such declaration of acceleration or dissolution or winding up or liquidation or reorganization, [3] any distribution of assets of the Obligor of any kind or character, whether in cash, property or securities, to which the holders of Junior Indebtedness would be entitled except for the provisions hereof, [4] shall be paid by the Obligor or by any receiver, trustee in bankruptcy, liquidating trustee, agent or other person making such payment or distribution, or by the holders of Junior Indebtedness if received by them, [5] directly to the holders of the Superior Indebtedness of the Obligor (pro rata to each such holder on the basis of the respective amounts of such Superior Indebtedness held by such holder), or their representatives to the extent necessary to pay all such Superior Indebtedness in full, in money, after giving effect to any concurrent prepayment or distribution to or for the benefit of the holders of such Superior Indebtedness, [6] before any payment or distribution is made to the holders of Junior Indebtedness.

Sorry about that, but no pain, no gain. The sentence may represent careful drafting, but it poses formidable difficulties for a reader. (My computerized grammar checker pronounced it readable at the 104th grade level.)

What can be done? There's no fun doing something easy, so I'm going to limit the possible improvements by assuming, for the moment, that nothing in the sentence is excessive; not a word can be left out without exposing a party to material legal risks. Now that we're assured of a rollicking good time, let's take a closer look at our beastie.

The beginning of the sentence up to the semi-colon before [2] has the structure: "Upon (i) or (ii), A before B." In a concession to the reader, the drafter has helpfully marked (i) and (ii). The difficulty, however, is finding the point where clause A begins (it's with the word "all" at [1]). We can, however, clearly indicate the shift from antecedent to consequent by simply indenting clauses (i) and (ii), as in:

Upon
- any payment being required to be made by the Obligor under the Junior Indebtedness upon any declaration of acceleration of the principal amount thereof or
- any payment or distribution of assets of the Obligor of any kind or character, whether in cash, property or securities, to creditors upon any dissolution or winding up or total or partial liquidation or reorganization of the Obligor, whether voluntary or involuntary or in bankruptcy, insolvency, receivership or other proceedings,

all principal, premium . . .

Now the first half of the sentence is easier to read, and we have a useful trick: *Indent the elements of a list.* The extent of the trick's usefulness may not be immediately apparent. Lists don't have to be numbered; any conjunction (and) or disjunction (or) is a candidate for such trickery. (I recently had some responsibility for an over 300-word sentence that, by extensive indenting, was made to surrender up its meaning without a struggle.)

We can use our new trick to indicate the two halves of our example sentence:

(a) Upon
   • any payment being required to be made by the Obligor under the Junior Indebtedness upon any declaration of acceleration of the principal amount thereof or
   • any payment or distribution of assets of the Obligor of any kind or character, whether in cash, property or securities, to creditors upon any dissolution or winding up or total or partial liquidation or reorganization of the Obligor, whether voluntary or involuntary or in bankruptcy, insolvency, receivership or other proceedings,
   [1] all principal, premium, if any, and interest due or to become due upon all the Superior Indebtedness of the Obligor shall first be paid in full, or payment thereof provided for in money, before any payment is made under Junior Indebtedness; [2] and
(b) upon any such declaration of acceleration or dissolution or winding up or liquidation or reorganization, ...

Unlike the "all" at [1] that begins the consequent in the first part of the sentence, there's little danger that a reader will overrun the semi-colon that divides the sentence before "[2]". Still, visually blocking out the logical structure of a sentence aids comprehension. I suspect that readers don't proceed linearly but constantly glance ahead to orient themselves (I know I do). If they can see where they are going, they will better understand where they are.

Sentences That Do Too Much

The second half of the sentence requires a different trick. The structure is set out as:

[2] and upon any such declaration of acceleration or distribution . . . [3] any distribution of assets of the

Obligor . . . [4] shall be paid . . . [5] directly to the holders of the Superior Indebtedness . . . [6] before any distribution is made to . . . .

This wouldn't be impossibly complicated were it not for the 33 words separating [4] from [5] and the 68 words between [5] and [6]. The reader is overwhelmed by verbiage well before he can discern the logical structure. How much better the world would be if the second half read as follows:

[2] *and upon any such declaration of acceleration or dissolution or winding up or liquidation or reorganization,* [3] *any distribution of assets of the Obligor* ~~of any kind or character, whether in cash, property or securities, to which the holders of Junior Indebtedness would be entitled except for the provisions hereof,~~ [4] *shall be paid by the Obligor* ~~or by any receiver, trustee in bankruptcy, liquidating trustee, agent or other person making such payment or distribution, or by the holders of Junior Indebtedness if received by them,~~ [5] *directly to the holders of the Superior Indebtedness* ~~of the Obligor (pro rata to each such holder on the basis of the respective amounts of such Superior Indebtedness held by such holder), or their representatives~~ *to the extent necessary to pay all such Superior Indebtedness in full,* ~~in money, after giving effect to any concurrent prepayment or distribution to or for the benefit of the holders of such Superior Indebtedness,~~ [6] *before any payment or distribution is made to the holders of Junior Indebtedness.*

Without blackline:

upon any such declaration of acceleration or dissolution or winding up or liquidation or reorganization, any distribution of assets of the Obligor shall be paid by the Obligor directly to the holders of the Superior Indebtedness to the extent necessary to pay all such Superior

Indebtedness in full before any payment or distribution
is made to the holders of Junior Indebtedness.

Not the clearest sentence ever penned but substantially less fog-
bound at 61 words than its 166-word progenitor. And, of course,
nothing will be lost *because* we shall add a new sentence that
reads:

In the preceding sentence,
- a "distribution of assets of the Obligor" means a distribution of assets of the Obligor of any kind or character,
  whether in cash, property or securities, to which the holders of Junior Indebtedness would be entitled except for the
  provisions hereof,
- "paid by the Obligor" means . . . .

The trick is to slim down the offending half-sentence by trans-
ferring most of its bulk to a second sentence. We trade an
incomprehensible half-sentence for one and a half comprehensible ones. The overall document is a bit longer, unless we can
use just one of those definitions again, which will shorten the
overall document.

Our second trick deserves more study. Note that the added
sentence doesn't define any new terms. Readers understand "distribution of the assets of the Obligor" without more; the added
sentence only states what the majority of readers would have nat-
urally understood the phrase to mean. It's a bit of legal hyper-
fastidiousness. So our second trick can be stated as: *It's okay to
explain at length what most people know, but do it somewhere else.*

For example, what's wrong with the following sentence?

If the Company registers any shares of its common stock
under the Securities Act of 1933, or any successor
statute, or the regulations promulgated by the Securities
and Exchange Commission (or any successor body)
thereunder, as then in effect, the Stockholder may, in its
sole discretion, at any time and from time to time,
request the Company to register not less than 250,000 of

the Shares under such Act, and the Company shall promptly comply with each such request.

From one point of view, nothing is wrong. The drafter has identified and resolved two potential ambiguities. First, the sentence makes it clear that registration is not limited to the Securities Act as currently in effect. Second, the drafter has removed any implication that the stockholder's registration rights are a one-time-only affair or that the Company has any right to object to a request.

Wait a minute. The drafter has removed the specified ambiguities but has also given the sentence a bad case of the meanders. Consider how much clearer the sentence was before our careful drafter decided to quadruple its comma allotment:

> If the Company registers any shares of its common stock under the Securities Act of 1933, ~~or any successor statute, or the regulations promulgated by the Securities and Exchange Commission (or any successor body) thereunder, as then in effect~~, the Stockholder may, ~~in its sole discretion, at any time and from time to time~~, request the Company to register not less than 250,000 of the Shares under such Act, and the Company shall promptly comply with each such request.

Without blackline:

> If the Company registers any shares of its common stock under the Securities Act of 1933, the Stockholder may request the Company to register not less than 250,000 of the Shares under such Act, and the Company shall promptly comply with each such request.

Lawyers often say that each sentence should be susceptible to only one interpretation. One imagines a judge years hence giving the longer sentence a careful reading and concluding that the stockholder may request a second registration under the rules promulgated by the Securities and Commodities Commission under the Financial Instruments Act of 2017. Surely the right result, but should every intervening reader suffer through the longer sentence when a judicial misreading is so unlikely? Most sentences aren't litigated, and a judge would probably do as well with the shorter sentence as the longer. Moreover, we can give our judge all the help he needs without turning every sentence into a maze.

The flaw in the longer sentence's approach is that it tries to handle all possible ambiguities within the sentence itself. However, the sentence is part of a document; therefore, ambiguities can be resolved elsewhere.[13] For example, suppose our judge could refer to a section near the end of the document that reads as follows:

> In this agreement, unless otherwise stated or the context otherwise requires, the following usages apply:
>
> - Actions permitted under this agreement may be taken at any time and from time to time in the actor's sole discretion.
> - References to a statute shall refer to the statute and any successor statute, and to all regulations promulgated under or implementing the statute or successor, as in effect at the relevant time.

You can imagine other provisions for this section that could help clear the undergrowth of legal prose, and I shall offer some additional provisions shortly. First, however, a general principle: If a reader will normally understand a simple sentence a certain way, or if a reader is unlikely to think of a set of complications that are in fact unlikely, the drafter can leave the sentence alone or tuck the precise explanation in the back. If, however, the reader is likely to take the wrong track in a two-meanings sentence, or is likely to ignore a real and present possibility, then the point should be addressed in the sentence or the immediate vicinity.

13. To say more at this point would require us to swim in some deep epistemological waters. But keep your Speedo handy because we're going to take that dip in "Untangling the Legal Sentence—Sentences and Truth" at 42.

A legal document should teach a reader how a transaction works. The best teaching follows the order of importance: First, outline and structure, then details, beginning with the most relevant. Documents should flow in the same way—make the general structure clear, then explain the details that people are likely to get wrong, and lastly confirm the details people usually get right.

It's easier to say than do, but let's at least do the simple part—put the unimportant stuff at the end. Here, for example, are a few more usages you can add at the end of the document:

- In computing periods from a specified date to a later specified date, the words "from" and "commencing on" (and the like) mean "from and including," and the words "to," "until" and "ending on" (and the like) mean "to but excluding."
- References to a governmental or quasi-governmental agency, authority or instrumentality shall also refer to a regulatory body that succeeds to the functions of the agency, authority or instrumentality.
- Indications of time of day mean [pick the city where most of your readers are] time.
- "A or B" means "A or B or both."
- "Including" means "including, but not limited to."

Our tricks are just applications of a basic rule: *Make the sentence structure clear.* It's not length that's at fault in our examples; it's length that obscures structure. A thousand crisply worded sentences do not raise the dust of a hundred convoluted ones. I've never read a legal document as long as *The Red and the Black,* but Stendhal is comprehensible whereas Messrs. Dewey, Cheatham & Howe are obscure.

If we make the structure of sentences, paragraphs and documents readily apparent, our readers will have a framework on which all those words can hang. Nothing we draft will be as memorable as Stendhal, but at least we shall give our readers documents they can understand. Who knows, we might save them time enough to take up *The Charterhouse of Parma.*

SAYING IT MORE THAN ONCE

In offering some tips for organizing the super-long sentences that continually pop up in legal documents, I proceeded on the assumption that every word was legally necessary. The task was then to organize all those words into a comprehensible structure.

The time has come to ask whether we need all those words. This is a big question, so I shall start with a more manageable one: Must we say anything more than once?

Consider the following passage from the subordination provisions example at the beginning of this chapter that so delighted us:

> . . . any payment or distribution of assets of the obligor
> of any kind or character, whether in cash, property or
> securities . . . .

The pattern is depressingly familiar: A universal ("any payment or distribution of assets of the obligor") is reprised ("of any kind or character") and then illustrated ("whether in cash, property or securities"). Would "any payment or distribution of assets of the obligor" alone have been enough?

Sometimes the extra words do real work and sometimes they don't. Not surprisingly, it helps to know some law. The words "so-and-so absolutely and irrevocably agrees that . . ." are usually blather, but "so-and-so absolutely and irrevocably guarantees . . ." may not be.[14] In our example, "of any kind or character" doesn't distinguish between "limited kind and character" subordinations and "unlimited kind and character" subordinations and may therefore be omitted.

Decisions about illustrations are more difficult. Our example starts with the all-embracing "any payment or distribution," which might suggest that illustrations are unnecessary. However, "any" doesn't mean "anything you could conceivably think of." Rather, "any" and "all" always mean something like "anything within the relevant context of discourse." For example, when we

---

14. I discuss the particular characteristics of guaranties in "Supporting Players—Guaranties" at 161.

speak of "any distribution," we do not countenance pillage. Additional words that help us determine the appropriate range of discourse can therefore be helpful. But when do we need such help?

There is no general answer, but there are easy cases. In our example, it is implausible that cash or securities would not be considered assets of the obligor. The context is subordination provisions and the intent is plain: The senior creditors want to be paid first. In the face of an intention so manifest, the illustrations in our example add little.

Contrast this example with another from that same enormous sentence: "all principal . . . and interest due or to become due" is to be paid to the senior creditors before any liquidating payment or distribution is made to the junior creditors. What does "due or to become due" add to "all principal and interest"?

In other cases, "due or to become due" might add little. Here, however, it serves a useful purpose. The general rule (which I haven't shown you) of the subject subordination provisions is that a payment cannot be made to a junior creditor if any payment *then due* to a senior creditor has not been made. The "due or to become due" in our example makes it clear that on a *liquidating* distribution, all principal and accrued interest—not just principal and interest currently due—must be paid to the seniors before the juniors receive anything. In this context, the extra phrase has work to do.

Note that "due or to become due" adds something because it counters a clear implication from another part of the document. We do not have to hypothesize a judge of profound obtuseness to find the extra words worth saying.

(This isn't a treatise on drafting subordination provisions, but I can't restrain myself from pointing out that the immense sentence we started with was too short as well as too long: It left out a critical clause. Under New York law, at least, if the senior lenders want to collect interest that accrues after the debtor files a bankruptcy petition, they have to say so expressly.[15])

15. *In re Southeast Banking Corp.*, 93 N.Y.2d 178 (1999).

Time for an objection: I counseled doing without the additional words "of any kind or character, whether in cash, property or securities" in the first passage discussed above. If the repetitions could conceivably be helpful, however, what is the harm in leaving them in?

Let's rephrase the objection because there's an important issue to address. Rephrased, the objection would be that discovering the appropriate context of discourse takes time, judgment and extensive legal knowledge. Wouldn't it be better, in most cases at least, to depend on a standard form that has been developed to take care of many contexts of discourse, albeit at some cost in conciseness?

I'm a believer in standard form agreements. The Public Securities Association (now the Bond Market Association) standard form repurchase agreement, for instance, has saved my clients an ocean of legal fees. Not all forms are so useful, however. Forms tend to grow by accretion, with many persons adding paragraphs and clauses without much understanding of what has gone before. The result is frequently a form whose numerous intricacies and subtleties are invisible to all sides.

The problem is that a statement's implications can only be understood in a context. We start off with a rough picture of the world in which the statement is made. As we fill in more information about that world, the meaning and implications of the statement change. Change the world, change the meaning.

The phenomenon is familiar. Every law student learns the game of analogize and distinguish. If you want this precedent to apply (or not apply) to these facts, add more facts. At reality's banquet, there will almost always be just those tidbits that, heaped onto the judge's plate, will make our precedent control or vanish as we wish.

In documents, we usually work on the conclusion rather than its factual premise. If, for example, a particular fact pattern carries the unwanted implication that only principal and interest currently due must be paid, we add "due or to become due" to the description of the amount to be paid. This is undoubtedly effective, but it tends to conceal the motivation for the provision.

There is no end to the possible situations that support awkward interpretations. As a result, lawyers often guard against extremely unlikely contexts. They conjure up nightmarish fact patterns and then add clauses to guard against the demons of their imaginings.

Some 20 years ago, Bayless Manning identified a "Law of Conservation of Ambiguity":

> Elaboration in drafting does not result in reduced ambiguity. Each elaboration introduced to meet one problem of interpretation imports with it new problems of interpretation.[16]

Think of a document as the instructions you need to get from *A* to *B*. Many things can go wrong with the facts on which the instructions are based, so it's sensible to add additional instructions as to what to do if a bridge is washed out, to point out additional landmarks in case the more prominent ones are destroyed, etc. Manning's point might be rephrased by saying that there is no end to such additional instructions. Moreover, after a point (quickly reached), extra instructions make it harder to find our way.

Against any proffered scenario, we have our own good sense as to whether the fact pattern is one that is worth guarding against. Against the unstated scenarios that motivated the provisions of a venerable form, however, we have fewer defenses. Documents usually present a lawyer's response to unstated scenarios. Unless we can work back to the facts a particular provision was designed to handle, we can't know whether the provision is a sensible response to a plausible scenario or is irrelevant to the concerns of the current transaction.

There is an enormous body of law, of which none of us knows more than a smattering. The temptation is strong to believe that if we leave out some bit of a document we don't

---

16. Bayless Manning, *Hyperlexis and the Law of Conservation of Ambiguity: Thoughts on Section 385*, 36 Tax Law. 9 (1982).

understand, we shall be visited with a legal catastrophe. Fear prevents us deleting bits that are no longer needed.

Courage! Most subtleties in legal documents aren't so subtle once you focus on them. There is a maxim in law, with which I hold, that you never pass up the chance to draft the documents. The reason is that the drafter understands the document better than the most thorough reader. A corollary must be that to better understand a venerated piece of legal boilerplate, you should try redrafting it. Understanding the legal implications of the document, not paying it obeisance, is how we should earn our keep.

So here's Dr Darmstadter's miracle diet: Every time you produce a document, rethink one sentence of the boilerplate. We can fight the battle against legal bloat one potato chip at a time. *Just do it!*

When Once Is Too Much

When it comes to readability, nothing beats a blank page. In the preceding section, I asked whether there was any reason for saying something more than once. Here I consider a more intriguing question: When can you say nothing?

I had cause to think about the uses of silence while drafting an agreement under which a group of banks would lend against securities held by a collateral administrator. Agreements for similar facilities went on for pages describing how the administrator would credit and debit collateral to various accounts. Most of these soporific paragraphs were near the front of the agreement, and my first thought was to move them to a schedule at the end. Then I realized that I could leave these paragraphs out altogether.

The number and types of collateral accounts and the movements of collateral between the accounts were important to the collateral administrator and the borrower because they affected the fees the borrower would pay the administrator. The fees were not to be disclosed to the lenders, however, so there was no reason for them to be concerned with the account mechanics. These matters could therefore be moved from the agreement to a confidential fee agreement between the borrower and the collateral administrator. All that needed to be stated in the main agreement was that the collateral administrator would hold the collateral in accounts for the benefit of the lenders. The details of the account structure went from an aggravation for all the parties to a *folie à deux* for borrower and administrator alone.

The benefit of saying nothing did not stop there. Once I focused on the account structure as a matter of fees, it became obvious that the account structure was dictated by the practices of the collateral administrator. All that was necessary for the fee agreement was to memorialize enough of those practices so that the fees could be calculated. This simplified the description of the account structure.

The agreement also required the collateral administrator to determine the market value of the collateral and how much could be loaned against it. Different types of collateral received different loan values. For example, more could be loaned against a treasury bill than against an investment grade corporate bond, and more could be loaned against a bond than against common stock. The percentage difference between the market value of a security and its loan value is commonly referred to as a "haircut."

I placed the specification of the haircuts in a schedule at the back of the agreement. This was a questionable decision: Haircuts are important for borrowers and lenders, and I generally favor putting important matters forward. I had, however, a linguistic reason for moving the haircuts to a schedule. The schedule entries looked like "US Treasuries—95%" and "Yankee bonds, investment grade—90%." Placed in a schedule, the language would be understood as the practical jargon of the markets. Placed in the body of the agreement, however, such phrases would inevitably raise the question: Should we define "Treasuries," "Yankee bonds," and so forth?

My own response to this type of question is perhaps the counsel of laziness: Leave it out unless there's a good reason to put it in. There are often good reasons for definitions. For example, some readers may wonder what a "Yankee bond" is. (It's a dollar-denominated security issued by a non-U.S. company and traded in the U.S.). But for the parties, the terms in the schedule had well understood meanings—they are part of the *argot* of the business. So definitions would not enlighten the participants. Moreover, definitions would entail the sort of anthropological exploration that can leave even the best legal drafter adrift in an alien culture. The result is often a set of rigid definitions that mis-describe the natives' practices. If a definition miscategorized a security, the agreement might have to be amended. Amending agreements to fix faulty definitions would embarrass the drafter (in this case, me) and annoy the parties (which included my employer).

Two observations on the preceding saga. First, moving material from the main agreement to a less formal schedule or side agreement is one way to scratch the legal itch to define every-thing. Second, lawyers' definitions of concepts that the nonlegal participants "feel in their bones" may be counter-productive. People who work with a concept every day are likely to see its application to a new situation better than a legal scrivener who only occasionally visits the neighborhood. Understanding a con-cept does not always mean knowing how to define it.

Even if we suppose the drafter's definitions accurately describe current practices, what has been gained? If the collateral administrator and the lender later differ as to the proper catego-rization of a security, the lawyer's rigid definition may settle the matter in a manner that seems arbitrary to the parties. Far better to let the participants come to their own resolution of the dis-agreement. Under my collateral agreement, for example, the col-lateral administrator is likely to be valuing securities every day. If on the 123rd day there is a dispute about some novel security or situation, all that may be necessary is for the administrator and the borrower to spend a few profitable minutes yelling at each other. The collateral administration agreement, like many other agreements, is between parties who have done business together before and intend to continue doing so. The participants can be trusted to react reasonably to unforeseen contingencies.

I hasten to say that the final form of the schedule of haircuts described above was not quite the rustic artifact that these reflec-tions might suggest. The lawyers refined the terminology and added explanations to resolve ambiguities. The lawyers did not, however, start with the view that every term needed defining. Rather, the lawyers addressed specific business problems that could be resolved by refining the schedule's wording.

Moving the specification of the haircuts to a schedule was, for me, a stratagem to evade the legal rage for definition. Definitions reduce uncertainty, but they also make the document brittle. As unanticipated situations arise, the rigid definitions may force outcomes undreamed of by the participants. The absence of definitions may allow the participants to work out a business solution without the necessity to first neutralize the agreement through waiver and amendment. The lawyer's job is not to explain all; it is to make that nice judgment as to what needs explaining and what does not. It's an art, not a science.

Nevertheless, lawyers frequently insist on defining well-understood trade terminology, often with disastrous results. Why? (Does anyone remember when we used to define "prime rate" as the rate the bank offered its most credit-worthy customers? Around 1980, class-action lawyers discovered that some customers were borrowing at less than prime, with the predictable unpleasant consequences for the banks.)

The desire to define all is merely a part of a more pervasive tendency—the attempt to address all contingencies. If the lawyers (or the businesspeople who buy into this approach) can dream up any scenario short of science-fiction, they assume the scenario must be addressed in the agreement. However, agreements that attempt to deal with remote and poorly understood contingencies are likely to misfire.

There is a big difference between real situations and the scenarios dreamed up months or years before. Events arrive full-blown, with all their factual background filled in. Sitting around a table dreaming up scenarios, we try to get the most important facts straight, but in many cases the facts we didn't consider turn out to be, cumulatively, determinative of the reasonable result. The contingency as it actually appears is described in the agreement, but it is critically different from the scenario in the drafter's mind.

Drafting an agreement, as I've stated earlier, is akin to giving a set of directions for finding your way through an unfamiliar country. The directions are only useful to the extent the person giving them knows the terrain. We send our travelers one way because we know the ground is flat and only later learn that it is also quicksandy. When we know the country well, we give precise directions ("Turn right at the second stoplight"). When the countryside is less familiar or less studded with identifiable markers, our directions must be more general ("Head toward the twin peaks for half a day").

So, our drafting strategy should be to carefully address the central concerns of the businesspeople involved; give precise directions for those contingencies that are well understood; give general and looser guidance for contingencies that are less well understood; don't try to solve every imaginable problem; trust the specialized knowledge of the parties.

FOOTNOTES

In an otherwise useful article, the author launched into her subject with the following sentence:

> As proposed in Investment Company Act Release No. 18736 (May 29, 1992) (the "Rule 3a-7 Proposing Release"), and adopted in Investment Company Act Release No. 19105 (November 19, 1992) (the "Rule 3a-7 Adopting Release"), Rule 3a-7 provides that an issuer of certain asset-backed securities would not be an investment company subject to regulation under the 1940 Act.

If you had trouble penetrating that sentence, there's a reason. The front end of the sentence is a sort of typographical breastwork, bristling with capital letters, parentheses and full height numerals, all defending citations that are of no interest to the general reader. With luck, the eye may skip over this 33-word fortification to alight on "Rule 3a-7 provides," which marks the true beginning of the sentence.

Citations are digressions from the main thought of the sentence. There's nothing wrong with digressions (I'm quite fond of parentheticals, for instance), but citations are digressions that interrupt rather than expand. You have no reason to read them until you are ready to go to the sources. Yet, we need citations. They keep authors honest and they provide a trail to the primary sources. How can we have citations without dead-end digressions and visual clutter?

The first step is to move the citations out of the body of the text and into footnotes or endnotes. Your eye must detour around citations in the body of the text, whereas citations in footnotes or endnotes can be ignored. Of course, citations in the main text have their occasional uses. For instance, in a judicial opinion, textual citations may add momentum to an onrushing syllogism, as in:

Major premise [citation]
Minor premise [citation]
Conclusion [BIG citation]

Still, for most purposes, the main text is the least desirable place for a citation. So why do legal writers (almost uniquely) insist on squeezing citations into the main text rather than relegating them to notes? The suspect in this case must be our stock villain, the typewriter. Using footnotes on a typewriter is sheer hell. (At some universities before the emergence of the word processor, doctoral dissertations had footnotes typed in the middle of the page, a simple but ugly concession to the limitations of the typewriter.)

Word processors make footnoting and endnoting simple, but old habits linger. I doubt that many people who casually tuck a citation into mid-sentence realize that they are obeying a technological edict that lapsed some 20 years ago.

OR ENDNOTES?

So what's it to be, footnotes or endnotes? Endnotes inflict the pain of constant flipping from text to endnote and back, but if we want to discourage readers from looking at citations, this pain can be our ally—not as good as electric shocks but effective nonetheless.

With footnotes, on the other hand, the eye need only travel up and down a single page. This is desirable if the footnotes contain textual material as well as citations. Placing a thought in a footnote clearly marks it as a digression, and a footnote enables an author to affect an ironic distance from her text. Used skillfully, footnotes can amuse and inform. Bear in mind, however, that too many trips up and down the page will impair readability.

A solution I have seen used effectively is to use footnotes *and* endnotes. The endnotes are numbered and consist solely of citations, done in a skeletal style (e.g., Holmes (1892), 23), buttressed by a full bibliography. The footnotes, which are infrequent, consist of nonbibliographic digressions, marked with asterisks (*) and daggers (†). Asterisks and daggers are easier to find on the page than numbers, and readers quickly learn to read the footnotes and ignore the endnotes.

INSERTING THE DAGGER

Where in the text should you place the number or other referent for a footnote or endnote? The worst place is the middle of a sentence; the best place is the end of a paragraph. Not only is there less interruption to the train of thought if the referent is at the paragraph's end, but it's also easier to regain your place in the text.

The end of the paragraph may be many words away from the proper place to reference the note. The note, however, can explain where it is to apply. Using this technique, several citations can be given in a single note. This limits the referents to one per paragraph. Without such a limit, referents can become a swarm of gnats distracting the reader from the text.

If you find such gnats annoying, you may be able to get rid of them entirely. In *The Guns of August,* Barbara Tuchman uses endnotes without gnats. The endnotes identified their subject matter by reference to the page and a snatch of text. This is a near perfect solution to the citation problem, for the text now provides no indication of the citation while still permitting anyone so inclined to easily track down the source. However, such a solution is difficult to effect. The page references in the endnotes have to be constantly adjusted as the text pagination changes, which can be difficult even with a modern word processor.

Tuchman's solution was nearly perfect. For true perfection, there is the approach Garrett Mattingly took in *The Armada:*

> Since this book is addressed not to specialists but to the general reader interested in history, there are no footnotes. But on the chance that some student of the period, turning these pages, might feel a bit of curiosity about the grounds for some judgment or assertion, I have appended a general account of the documents and printed books most relied on, followed by short notes on the chief sources for each chapter, with special reference to the evidence for any views which depart from those generally accepted.[17]

Mattingly's solicitousness for his readers caused him to forgo the customary scholarly apparatus. Of course, when you're Garrett Mattingly, they cut you some slack. Steeled by Mattingly's example, I will now decline to give the page number for the quotation. As another historian, of a different period and subject matter, has counseled, "You could look it up" (citation omitted).

Parentheticals

Recent SEC comment letters on filed prospectuses have often contained this "plain English" comment:

> Eliminate parenthetical phrases throughout your document. Parenthetical phrases are a legalistic convention that disrupt the flow of information. . . . If the information in

---

17. GARRETT MATTINGLY, THE ARMADA (1959).

parentheses is important enough to be included in the disclosure, include it in its own sentence or set it off with commas or dashes in the same sentence.

Before going further, let us straighten out our terminology. My old Webster's Collegiate says that a parenthetical is "of the nature of a parenthesis" and that a parenthesis is:

A word, phrase, or sentence, by way of comment or explanation, inserted in, or attached to, a sentence grammatically complete without it. It is usually marked off with a curved line, commas, or dashes.

By *parenthetical,* however, the SEC clearly means a parentheses marked off with curved lines, and I will generally use the term with that sense here.

Since you've gotten this far, you have no doubt noticed that I use a lot of parentheticals. It's not something I'm proud of, and I've resolved—despite the evidence in these pages—to use fewer of them. I have no intention, however, of doing away with parentheticals altogether. I think I'm in good company. Consider the following:

It is now necessary to warn the writer that his concern for the reader must be pure: he must sympathize with the reader's plight (most readers are in trouble about half the time) but never seek to know his wants.

I don't think these guys are doing something wrong. (Lest I be chided for using sexist language, they are in fact guys—William Strunk, Jr. and E.B. White, as it happens.)[18]

Parentheticals are disruptive, but disruption has its uses. My first parenthetical in this section (which is set off by dashes) is a humorous disruption—at least, that was the intention. A second me is interrupting to offer delightfully mocking comment on the primary me. Don't you love it?

18. STRUNK & WHITE, ELEMENTS OF STYLE 85 (3d ed. 1979).

My Strunk & White parenthetical, however, is rigged as a booby-trap. The reader walks in expecting a minor interruption, and the bomb detonates—the perpetrators of the quoted parenthetical are not just any two guys. (In case you didn't know, Strunk & White's little book is one of the holy texts of plain English.)

So parentheticals have their uses. But are they useful in *prospectuses?* I recently trekked through a couple of prospectuses, stopping at each parenthetical to ask if it was necessary. The sample was neither large nor random but instructive nonetheless.

Many of the parentheticals introduced defined terms or were cross-references to other parts of the prospectus. All the other parentheticals were either exceptions or amplifications. Amplifications give additional information. They often start with words like "and," "including" or "which." For example:

A specified undivided interest in the trust assets in the initial amount of $ ____ (which amount represents ___ % of the sum of the initial invested amount) constitutes credit enhancement for the certificates.

Exceptions qualify a more general statement in the sentence. Exceptions often begin with words like "if," "excluding," "unless," "provided," "or in the case of," "subject to," "other than," "after giving effect to" or "but only to the extent that." For example,

The certificates include the right to receive (but only to the extent needed to make payments of interest on each interest payment date at the applicable certificate rate) varying percentages of the collections of finance charge receivables.

Obviously, these parentheticals were not inserted for any comic or other literary effect. They're long (and were longer in the originals), they're plunked down in the middle of the sentence, they're . . . disruptive. I don't think anything would be gained by replacing these parentheses with commas or dashes, however. Commas might only make things worse.

A left parenthesis brings things to a stop, but it does have one nice feature: For every left parenthesis there is an equally obtrusive right parenthesis that signals the end of the disruption. The same can be said of dashes, which often travel in noisy pairs. Commas, in contrast, quietly occur at many places in a sentence, so you may miss the comma that signals the end of a disruption.

Moreover, commas or dashes might shift the emphasis in unintended ways. As Richard Wydick points out:

> Commas, parentheses, and dashes . . . differ in the emphasis they give to the material they set off. Commas tend to be neutral; they neither emphasize nor play down the material. Parentheses tend to play down the material, to make it clearly subordinate. Dashes tend to emphasize the material.[19]

The problem with our examples, however, is not how the disruption is marked but the disruption itself. Consider the following example:

> Interest will accrue from the preceding interest payment date (or in the case of the first interest payment date, from the closing date) to the next interest payment date.

Logically, the sentence has the form "Interest will accrue from the first interest payment date or the closing date to the next interest payment date." Our drafter, quite sensibly, did not state it that way because the two disjuncts—the preceding interest payment date and the closing date—are not on a par. The preceding interest payment date will happen again and again, but the closing date will only happen once. The closing date is a true exception to the general rule and, consequently, was placed in an exception parenthetical. If the closing date is

---

19. RICHARD C. WYDICK, PLAIN ENGLISH FOR LAWYERS 98 (4th ed. 1998).

an exception, however, it should wait until *after* the statement of the general rule. The best place for the disruption is the next sentence:

> Interest will accrue from the preceding interest payment date to the next interest payment date. For the first interest payment date, interest will accrue from the closing date.

Our other two examples would also best be handled by moving the disruption to a following sentence. If the parenthetical is short, however, setting it off with commas may work, as in the following three examples:

1. . . . a percentage (either 2% or 3%) of the outstanding balance . . . .
2. The Company (through its predecessor) is . . . .
3. . . . the trust will not be deemed to be an association (or publicly traded partnership) taxable as a corporation.

Symptomatic relief of parentheticalitis is fairly straightforward, but a real cure requires us to understand the cause of the disease. When a general statement is subject to an exception or two, why do drafters feel that the exceptions must be packed into the same sentence as the general statement?

For many drafters, the unit of truth is the sentence. For them, the preceding examples, shorn of their protective exceptions, would just be *false*. On this line of reasoning, each sentence must be true taken by itself—that is, its truth or falsity cannot be allowed to depend on some other sentence or sentences. (Perhaps this view stems from fear that any single sentence might be torn from its context by a plaintiff's lawyer.)

Such a position is, of course, ridiculous. Take our sample sentence, with its exception for the closing date. Reading the sentence by itself, how do you know what the closing date is, what an interest payment date is, and what, indeed, interest is being paid on?

The unit of truth is not the sentence but some larger structure, larger even than the prospectus. Much of what is said in a prospectus only makes sense against our present needs and our background knowledge—necessarily incomplete—of how the world works.

SENTENCES AND TRUTH

In the preceding section, I argued that each sentence in a prospectus is true or false only in the context provided by the entire prospectus as well as the background knowledge and goals of the anticipated reader. This is fairly abstract, so before we drift away in speculation, let's moor ourselves to a nonlegal example.

One of Newton's laws is that force equals mass multiplied by acceleration, usually written $F = ma$. Most of us have little idea what that equation means, even if we know that it's important. If we knew more physics, and could remember our college calculus, we could use it for all sorts of useful purposes. We could, for example, predict the tides and the motions of the planets.

The equation $F = ma$ is an important truth, but its importance and its truth depend on the rest of the Newtonian system—the other laws of motion and gravitation and the calculus. Even with the rest of the system, however, it's only true in some contexts. For calculating the orbits of the planets, it's super—unless you happen to be interested in precise predictions of the perihelion of Mercury. In that context, Newton's laws are false, and something else—relativity theory—turns out to be true (for us, for now).

You didn't learn this stuff in law school? OK, here's a brief history of modern physics: In the late 17th century, Isaac Newton came up with laws of motion and gravitation and a mathematical technique, the calculus, that explained and predicted the motions of earthly bodies—falling apples, artillery shells, the tides—as well as the planets and their moons as part of a single unified system. Early in the 20th century, Einstein showed that Newton's laws aren't quite right, and that the errors become larger as bodies move at higher speeds or in stronger gravitational fields. For example, when Mercury makes its closest approach to the Sun (its *perihelion*), the light rays from Mercury to us, passing close to the Sun's strong gravitational field (the Sun is BIG!), bend. (Actually, I'm told it's the space the rays pass through that bends—relativity is strange!)

So here's how you write a textbook on mechanics for engineers (I'm not a physicist or an engineer, but I'm a lawyer, so I have the right to be an expert): You start with Newton's laws—you can assume the students already know calculus—without the complexities that air resistance, friction and a host of other real-world considerations would raise. You give lots of examples and exercises until you feel that a diligent student will understand how to apply the Newtonian system. Then, one by one, you add air resistance, friction and other complexities. You never mention relativity theory. For an engineer, it's irrelevant.

A prospectus is a textbook: You're trying to explain to someone (an investor) how something (a security) works. As in any textbook, the truth of what you say depends on your audience. Each sentence in a prospectus is true or false only as part of the structure of the prospectus and a set of loosely understood assumptions about what the prospectus reader needs to know. And, as in our engineering textbook, you can, and you *should,* leave out exceptions that are not relevant to your investors' needs.

For example, in writing a prospectus for certificates backed by credit card receivables, I had to explain how the receivables were allocated to the certificates. The allocation is done by allocating the total pool of receivables among the different series of certificates, then taking the amount allocated to each series and allocating it between the investors and the sponsor. Two-steps. When I looked at the arithmetic, however, the process was: First, each series is allocated a portion of the receivables equal to a/b, and, second, the investors in the series are allocated a portion of that amount equal to b/c. High school algebra tells you that the investors are therefore allocated a portion of the receivables equal to a/c—one-step.

When I drafted the allocations as a one-step process, however, the other lawyers were unhappy. They didn't question my math, and they admitted that the reasons for the two-step process were of little interest to investors. But, they said, the allocations are, in fact, calculated by the two-step procedure. I couldn't convince them that my description of a one-step procedure was as true as it had to be. Eventually, we compromised on presenting a one-step process in the body of the prospectus, with the two-step procedure in an appendix. (When I seize power, that appendix will be among the first to be shot.)

Another example we're now familiar with is the brief history of physics I gave a few paragraphs back, which is ludicrously inadequate (and inaccurate) for most purposes. But for this book, it's as true as it needs to be.

We're so accustomed to the idea that you only have to say what you have to say that I shouldn't have to give any more examples. It's only when we stop thinking about what the audience needs to know and start worrying about Truth, in either the philosophical or the 10b-5 sense, that philosophers and lawyers tend to lose their bearings.

One of the reasons I had trouble convincing the other lawyers involved with the prospectus was that we had different ideas of the audience for the prospectus. For those veterans, the audience was a group of sophisticated investors who, they said, would want to see the allocations described the way they had always been described. For me, however, there would be no need for the prospectus if you could assume that your audience already knew it all.

But who is the prospectus audience? Until we know, it's difficult to say what disclosure is appropriate. If you're writing a prospectus, you have to make decisions about what to say and how to say it, and these decisions can't be made without some assumptions about your audience. There's little to guide you, however, and there are many openings for second-guessing by the plaintiffs' bar. All you can do is try to pitch your presentation to the "average investor" for the securities involved. If you happen to know that guy, I'd like to ask her a few questions.

THE LOOK OF THE DOCUMENT

Even though we have relieved some of the mindstrain caused by legalisms, we still must treat the eyestrain produced by the typical legal document. None of the subjects of this chapter are taught in law school, and few are learned in legal practice. I researched most of the technical matters at the public library. Considering these matters will provide some interesting instances of the failure of the legal profession to appreciate technological advances.

TIMES V. COURIER

The first rule in creating legal documents is: Use Times!

Times is a family of typefaces. By a "family" I mean the normal typeface plus *italic,* **bold** and ***bold italic***, each in various type sizes.

This paragraph is printed in Times. It probably looks to you a good deal like the typeface for the rest of the book (a typeface called Berkeley).

```
The paragraph in Times looks very dif-
ferent from this paragraph, which is printed
in a typeface called Courier. Courier is
derived from typewriters and should look
familiar.
```

There are thousands of other typefaces, and choosing the proper one for any particular document is a task for professionals. Thankfully, you can forget about the complications. For lawyers, there are usually only two choices: Courier and Times. Courier is always the wrong choice.

How can I be so sure? Because I have conducted thousands of experiments. The simplest of my experiments you can conduct yourself: Open the last book, magazine or newspaper that you read. It will almost certainly be printed in a typeface that looks more like Times than like Courier.

This is no accident. Publishers of books, magazines and newspapers want them to be read. They spend a lot of time considering what typefaces will encourage readership. None of them choose Courier.

So why do lawyers so frequently produce documents in Courier? Because they've always done so. As recently as 15 years ago, the only way to produce a legal document (short of sending it out to be printed) was on a typewriter or a daisy-wheel printer. The only typefaces available for that technology were typefaces like Courier. Lawyers have simply failed to react appropriately to the change from inked-ribbon printing to laser printing.

A typewriter (like its computerized cousin, the daisy-wheel printer) produces each individual letter with a metal letter form at the end of a hammer (or a ball or daisy-wheel) that strikes an inked ribbon onto a sheet of paper. The typewriter then moves the paper one space to prepare for the next letter impression. The mechanical characteristics of the typewriter place two important limitations on the shapes of the letters.

First, because the typewriter advances the paper a set distance no matter which letter is imprinted, all the letters are the same width. In contrast, you will notice that, in the last word of the preceding sentence, "width," the "w" is a good bit wider than the "i," the "d" has an in-between width, and the "t" is narrower than the "d" but wider than the "i." This typeface (Berkeley, as I pointed out earlier) is said to be "proportional," in contrast to Courier, which is said to be "monospaced." In Courier, "width" looks like "width," with each letter of equal width.

In Times and other proportional typefaces, the variations in width and height of letters ease the process of reading. If you don't believe me, consider the following:

A LITTLE PUZZLE

Here is a fun little teaser to impress upon you how much we depend on word shapes to read. On the following lines are two well-known proverbs. The letters are indicated only by black rectangles the size of each letter. Can you read the sentences? How quickly would you be able to read the words if they were set this way in all caps?

1.

2. [20]

The second effect of the typewriter on letters is caused by the limitations of the metal letter form. To reliably produce each letter, the metal ridges of the letter must be narrow enough not to diffuse the impact with the ribbon yet broad enough not to be worn down by constant striking. Consequently, the lines that form typed letters are all of the same thickness. You may not be conscious of it, but most printed text uses lines that vary in thickness. Compare for example, the double-sized words below, the one on the left in Times, and the one on the right in Courier:

Typeface Typeface

Note in Times how much thicker the vertical bar of the capital T is than the horizontal bar, how the curved part of the "p" billows out as it becomes vertical, and the varying thickness of

---

20. ROBIN WILLIAMS, THE PC IS NOT A TYPEWRITER 28 (1992). Reprinted with permission. *See also* ROBIN WILLIAMS, THE NON-DESIGNER'S DESIGN BOOK (1994). Both books should be required reading for every legal drafter.

the lines that form the "y," "c" and "e." All of these variations help your eye as it runs across the page.

To all of these considerations, the practice of law has turned a blind eye. Although every church group, garden club and drinking society in the country has seized the opportunities presented by word processing programs and laser printers to print its newsletters in an unseemly riot of typefaces, a (shrinking) majority of lawyers continue to use Courier. It is perhaps the most obvious example of the legal profession's refusal to adapt to technological change. Imagine if the medical profession, refusing to follow mere fashion, delayed using penicillin for 15 years?

So, proportional typefaces by all means, but why Times? First, you already have it. Times is built into almost every laser printer ever made. Times comes in a number of variants (e.g., Times Roman, CG Times, Times New Roman), and any of them is better than Courier.

Because you and all your friends already have Times, it gets used a lot. Consequently, it never looks precious. Times is already a legal workhorse. There's a reason for Times' ubiquity, however. It was originally designed in the 1930s for *The Times* (of London), although that newspaper has since changed typefaces. Newspapers cram a lot of words on a page and are printed with cheap ink on cheap paper. A newspaper typeface must therefore be compact yet readable under adverse conditions. Times is famously legible in the smallest sizes, attractive in large sizes (headings, for example) and stands up to photocopying and other forms of abuse.

SANS SERIF TYPEFACES

If you get interested in typefaces, you may be tempted to use the modernistic sans serif typefaces such as Helvetica, Univers and Arial that are likely to be packaged with your printer or word processor. **(A sentence in Univers, for example, looks like this.)** *Sans serif* is French for "without serifs," serifs being the little squiggles at the ends of the lines that make up a letter—at the top and bottom of the vertical line in the lower case "d," for example.

There's debate about whether sans serif type is harder to read. I understand that it's used a lot in France, and the French supposedly don't have any trouble with it. But then, have you ever driven a French car? We can settle the controversy, for our purposes, with two observations:

- No one argues that sans serif type is *easier* to read than serif type.
- Few magazines, newspapers or books are printed in sans serif type.

Until you develop some feeling for typefaces, the safest course is to use Times.

SIZE MATTERS!

What size Times should you use? Type is measured in *points,* there being 72 points to an inch. For everything but headings (which should be larger) or tables (which can be smaller), the choices range from 10 point to 12 point. (The type you are reading is 11 point.) Within these limits, if it looks too big (or too small), make it smaller (or bigger). Trust yourself.

AND SO DOES LENGTH

Time for the second rule in creating legal documents: Shorten your line! (In the publishing world, this is referred to as the "measure.")

The page size that we work with is invariably 8½ inches wide and 11 inches long; I'll call it the "standard page." The margins used by most typists and the default margins in many word processing programs (i.e., the margins you get unless you change them) are one inch. This means that, unless indented, text will stretch 6½ inches across the standard page, a distance I'll call a "standard line."

Text designers have a rule of thumb that, for easy reading, a line of text should not be longer than 1½ to two alphabets, or 39 to 52 characters. A standard line in Courier is 2½ alphabets—

only slightly outside the recommended range. A standard line in 10-point Times, however, stretches a full 4¼ alphabets. Even 12-point Times (the largest practicable size for document work) runs 3¼ alphabets to the standard line. This is probably part of the reason most books are published on pages substantially smaller than the standard page. Magazines are published on paper comparable to the standard page, but with the text broken into two or three columns.

The point is that the more words you cram on a line, the harder it is to find the next line. The number of words on a line increases as you lengthen the line and shrink the type. Six inches of Courier is too long (think of the times when you've had to read a document with a ruler under the line just to follow from one line to the next), and 12-point Times is smaller than Courier. Readability requires lines of a reasonable length. There's no hard and fast rule, but four inches of 12-point Times is surely not too short, and six inches is surely too long.

Despite its awkwardness for the computer age, we are probably stuck with the standard page. Luckily, for most documents, there are two good ways to shorten line length on a standard page. First, you can lay the document out like a term sheet, with headings in a narrow column on the left and the rest of the text in a column of four inches or less on the right. The term sheet format is easy to read, so why not use it for other documents? Lots of white space on a page enhances readability.

If you don't want all that white space, you can try a second solution: columns. This is the solution adopted by magazines printed on paper with dimensions close to the standard page. With most word processing programs, columns present few obstacles.

Still, not every document lends itself to either the term sheet format or to columns. The worst problems are caused by the simple business letter. These are usually done on letterhead, and large organizations often have style books dictating line lengths of six inches or more.

Of course, many letters are so short that readability isn't a concern. However, if the letter is long and intricate, such as a "reasoned" legal opinion, action may be necessary.

Some letterhead pushes you in the right direction. For example, charitable organizations often have the names of their prestigious boards of directors running down a column on the left side of the page. This forces a left margin (from the edge of the page) of at least two inches, which gives you a head start on a reasonable line length. If you're not so lucky, you can drop a vertical line down the page about one inch from the left side of the page and then treat the line as the effective edge. It makes the shorter line look more natural. You can also adopt my personal solution of simply using two-inch margins left and right and to hell with what people think. (Once I got used to them, I decided that the wide margins looked quite handsome). But in any case, shorten that line!

BETWEEN THE LINES

And now another (little) rule: Control the space between the lines! In printer's jargon, the space between lines is called the leading, pronounced *lehd-ing,* and I'll use that terminology here.

Few people appreciate how important leading is to readability. Fewer still realize that leading can be easily controlled in most word processing programs.

Little changes in leading make a big difference in readability. For example, in most word processing programs, single-spaced text will usually have about two points of leading for 10- or 12-point Times. In the publishing biz, 10-point type with two points of leading is said to be "set 10 on 12," usually written 10/12. You may think 10/12 looks just fine, and it often does, but going to 10/13—that is, adding one measly point of leading—makes the text lighter to the eye. Lighter text is easier to read.

Using Times, short lines set in columns and an extra dollop of leading can produce astonishing results. For example, *The Atlantic Monthly* was, until recently, printed in Times in two columns, each slightly over three inches wide set 10/13. *The Atlantic* is well written (for my taste), and the format adds to its readability. Its pages are attractive and seldom appear dense or crammed. Yet when I laid out a page on my word processor with the same format, it contained almost 1,000 words. Clearly, you can cram a great many words on one page without sacrificing a readable format.

Marking Your Paragraphs

Although there is much to be gained by expanding the space between lines, there is little to be gained by expanding the space between paragraphs. Leaving space between paragraphs is another hangover from typewriter technology. If you don't believe me, try to find a book or magazine that routinely leaves blank lines between paragraphs.

The universal symbol for a new paragraph is an indentation of the first line. See, for example, this paragraph.

A word processor can be made to indent the first line of a new paragraph automatically. On a typewriter, the trick was accomplished by hitting a tab key, and modern keyboards and word processors have preserved the tab key because we are used to doing it that way.

The typewriter experience has left another awkward remnant in legal documents: The first line indentations in legal documents are almost always one-half or one full inch. Even one-half inch is too large.

Here we go again. Pull out the last magazine or book you were reading and look at the first line indentations. They will almost certainly be a quarter-inch or less. I'm not sure why typed material used larger indentations, but I can guess. For one thing, typewriters normally were used to produce lines of six inches or more, so a half-inch indent might have been necessary to make the paragraph breaks stand out. Also, typed text is so difficult to read that it was frequently double-spaced. Double-spacing may require a more aggressive indentation to reliably signal the beginning of a new paragraph. If you're using Times on appropriately short lines, you won't need or want a first line indentation of more than a quarter-inch. Also, if it's clear from the context that you are starting a new paragraph—for example, immediately following a section heading or a space left between sections—you can dispense with the first-line indentation altogether, as I do in the first paragraph of each titled section.

EMPHASIS AND OVER-EMPHASIS

By statutory mandate or general expectation, certain information in a document is supposed to be conspicuous—certain statements in Securities Act prospectuses,[21] disclaimers of warranties in contracts for the sale of goods[22] and contractual choices of non-Texas law,[23] for example.

The typewriter offers only two ways to make text conspicuous: capitalization and underlining. Laser printing gives more options, including larger, contrasting, bold or italic type or shaded and enclosed text.

What difference does it make? Well, "conspicuous" and "readable" are not synonymous. In many cases, they are antithetical. For example, small type stands out but does not communicate well. When someone yells at us or whispers, we may have a hard time understanding what is being said even as we grasp that it is supposed to be important. Making text conspicuous *and* readable is no simple task.

(Most days as I walk to work, there's a guy standing on the center island in the middle of Park Avenue screaming something. I've been walking by him for years, his voice quite audible. I haven't the least idea what he's yelling about.)

Most of us realize that underlined text is hard to read. You've probably discovered that for yourself when you had to read a blacklined paragraph. You can read books and magazines for an entire year without encountering so much as a single underlined word. Underlined text is another example of an accommodation to the typewriter's limited repertoire.

Placing text in all capital letters is more common. The SEC once required capitalized text for certain statements on the front and inside front covers of a prospectus, and other cautions in a

21. Regulation S-K § 501.
22. U.C.C. § 2-316(2).
23. Oh, look it up.

prospectus are often capitalized. I have seen prospectuses with well over a page of all capitalized ("all caps") text.

All caps text is still another holdover from typewriter technology and is also difficult to read. The large quantity of ink that capital letters deposit on the page screams at us (POL CAUGHT IN LOVE NEST!), but longer stretches of capitalized text are often skipped over. No newspaper, book or magazine uses all caps for anything but headings. The reasons are easy to understand. Unlike lower case letters, capitals are all the same height. Printed capitals are also more similar in width than lower-case letters. Being so similar, they are hard to distinguish. Confronted with all caps text, the eye tends to wander. Even if we force ourselves to pay close attention, reading speed is reduced, and this change to the normal rhythm of reading reduces comprehension.

If text must be capitalized, you can improve readability somewhat by increasing the leading. Because all capital letters are tall, they appear to be packed closer to the lines above and below, which further increases the difficulty of reading all caps text. Increasing the leading as little as one or two points can be a big help.

If all caps are not required and a paragraph or less must be conspicuous, you can make text stand out by using larger print. Or you can enclose the paragraph in a box, a method I prefer. You can also use bold face for a sentence or less.

The foregoing suggestions are, however, only stop-gaps. Getting a reader to focus on a particular bloc of text is not easy. Luckily, anyone who wants to pursue the matter will find that instruction is not only available, it is ubiquitous.

Look at your daily newspaper. Text is made conspicuous by the simplest of means: The most important stories are on page one, the most important story on page one is on the right under the main headline, and the importance of the main story is signaled by the size of the headline and the number of columns devoted to it. The text itself is left alone: no all caps text, no larger or contrasting type, no italics and no boldface. A great deal of thought has gone into making this text as readable as possible, given the economics of newspaper printing.

We can learn some simple tricks from newspapers: Call attention to stories with headings; place important stories as close to the front as possible; don't monkey with the text. We can also learn a deeper truth.

Why do newspapers, but not novels, have headlines? Presumably because we expect to read everything in a novel but not everything in a newspaper. Newspapers are designed for ease of nonreading. The organization of the newspaper (front page, sports page, business page), the eye-catching headlines and even the organization of the individual stories (e.g., the who-what-where-when lead sentence) are designed to help us find what we want to read and to avoid what we don't want to read. Such organization in a novel would be self-defeating.

Reading is consensual. Nothing in a legal document is as calculated to grab your attention as the advertisements in the morning newspaper, yet you read few of them. You see them all—the energy, talent and low cunning devoted to advertising are not wasted—but you ignore almost all the text because you usually aren't interested.

Reflecting on newspapers yields several conclusions: First, there is no reason to make text conspicuous if it is bound to be read. Absent statutory mandate, a negotiated agreement does not need the text of a choice of law, arbitration or waiver of jury clause to be handled differently than the text of any other provision.

Second, you can call a provision to a reader's attention, but you cannot get him to read it. So capitalizing, bolding or doing anything else to a long passage of text is probably counterproductive. Even readers who would be interested may be less likely to read it to the extent it reduces readability. If you think that there are a hundred or more words that every reader should read, even if she reads nothing else, then put them up front under an eye-catching headline and hope for the best.

Finally, you can't make everything conspicuous. Being conspicuous is a matter of contrast—objects are conspicuous against a background of less conspicuous objects. So making any text conspicuous makes other text less conspicuous. As evidence, consider the mad jumble on the front page of an old-style

securities prospectus. It looked like the Surgeon General's warning run amok, and was probably read about as frequently. As Mr.
Justice Gilbert put it,

> When everyone is somebodee,
> Then no one's anybody.[24]

PROMISCUOUS CAPITALIZATION

We lawyers love definitions, and our documents bristle with
defined terms. Today's standard practice is to mark every occurrence of a defined term by capitalizing the first letter. The result
is that legal documents contain lots of words that begin with capital letters.

A word that begins with a capital carries an emphasis that it
would not normally have. The emphasis is helpful when it marks
the beginning of a sentence or emphasizes a word intended to be
emphasized. However, loading up sentences with capital letters
often lays stress on words that are not intended to be stressed and
impairs readability. When we read many pages crammed with
capitalized defined terms, the cumulative drag can be significant.

How can I be so sure that capitalization impairs readability?
There is a large amount of literature on page design and typogra-
phy, but it is hardly a science. Descriptions in such literature of
typefaces and their relative readability often sound like descriptions of the merits of fine wines—there is a marked emphasis on
the subjective. Still, there is evidence. Most notably, printed nontechnical materials generally shy away from capitalization. In
books and periodicals that aim for a large audience, defined
terms are seldom capitalized. (An alternative title for this book
might be "Look Around!")

But, you say, in German all nouns are capitalized. Do Germans have a tougher time reading than non-Germans? There are
several possible ripostes to this argument. For example, Germans
do have a tougher time reading (that's why they need six weeks
vacation a year), or Germans are tough (they can read Gothic

---

24. W.S. GILBERT, THE GONDOLIERS, act 2.

script). More convincingly, there may be no problem of misemphasis in German because *all* nouns are capitalized; difficulties only arise where some terms are capitalized but not others.

In any case, the question is not whether Germans have a tougher time with their capitalized nouns than we do with our lower-cased ones. The question should be: Are people like us, who are used to the limited use of capitalized words, likely to have trouble reading text where capitals are sprinkled more freely? It's no answer—at least it's not an answer I shall countenance—that we can get used to promiscuous capitalization. My audience is made up largely of nonlawyers. They should be able to read my documents with as few hindrances as possible.

We don't have to capitalize defined terms. The Uniform Commercial Code, like most statutes, does not capitalize defined terms, even though many of these terms (e.g., "fault" and "person") may have somewhat different meanings in nontechnical English. Capitalization can tell the world "I am a defined term," but that is not usually necessary.

The problems caused by over-capitalization may have been more manageable in legal documents printed in Courier or other monospaced typefaces. As discussed earlier, the mechanics of a typewriter require capital letters to have the same width and thickness as lower case letters. In print typefaces such as Times, however, capital letters are wider and composed with thicker lines than lower-case letters. In these typefaces, capitals throw more ink on the page than lower-case letters.

The relative equality of capital and lower-case letters in typed copy may explain why typists are taught to leave two spaces between the period that ends a sentence and the capital letter that starts the next. Because typed capital letters are similar in size and weight to typed lower-case letters, the extra space may be needed to help the eye find the beginning of the sentence. Printed materials, however, seldom leave more than one letter-space between sentences, probably relying on the greater bulk of the capital to signal the beginning of the sentence. If you've been leaving two spaces after a period in typefaces such as Times, you can stop now.

What all this means is that, in Courier, capitalized terms play softly. Switching to Times or a similar typeface turns up the volume considerably with results that may be cacophonous. The moral is not that we should stick with Courier, whose baleful effects on eye and spirit I have exhaustively documented, but that we should adjust our habits to take advantage of new opportunities. Unless there is a reason to capitalize a defined term—and there seldom is—don't do it.

On this point, I must admit, I have encountered resistance. Even my nonlawyer audience has insisted that defined terms be capitalized. The worry apparently is that the reader will not realize that a term has been defined to have a nonstandard meaning.

The quick answer is not to give a standard term a nonstandard meaning.[25] In the meantime, I have been gradually weaning my audience from capitalized defined terms by lowercasing all those defined terms whose definitions are fairly standard. For example, I now write "this agreement" rather than "this Agreement," "taxes" rather than "Taxes," and "affiliate" rather than "Affiliate."

If capitalized terms impair readability, all-capital terms are worse. For example, some documents use all capitals for defined terms. I think most people appreciate that these terms disrupt the flow of text. But what can you do with terms like ERISA or SIPC or FDIC that must be capitalized? Well, you can do what I just did, and what most printed materials do: Use small capitals. (The typographers' preference for small capitals provides additional evidence that capitals are disruptive.[26])

The small capitals used in word processing programs are scaled down capital letters and are not altogether satisfactory. The scaling-down makes the lines too thin so that a small caps word tends to stand out as a fainter patch of type on the page. Still, an all small-caps word is better than an all full-caps word. If you want real small caps, the kind printers use, you can obtain computerized real small caps for Times and most other popular typefaces.

25. *See* "Words—Naming and Mis-Naming" at 12.
26. *See, e.g.,* ROBERT BRINGHURST, THE ELEMENTS OF TYPOGRAPHICAL STYLE 45 (1992).

I've been speaking of capital letters, but in Times and similar typefaces, numerals function much like capitals—they throw a lot of ink on the page and tend to disrupt readability. Unfortunately, not much can be done, at least not easily. I've experimented with reducing the point size of numerals, and the results have been positive in appearance, but the process is too tedious to be practical.

The solution adopted by some typographers is to use lower case numerals, which, like real small caps, are available for Times and other popular typefaces. Regular numerals have the same height and width to facilitate their use in columns and other tabular work; lower case numerals are of varying width and heights. If you have access to lower case numerals, try them. If you don't, don't worry. Unless you use many, many numerals in your text, this problem is too minor to cause much fretting.[27]

JUSTIFICATION

It takes less time to state the general rule for justification than to explain what justification is, so I'll start at the end: Justification hardly ever matters, so do whatever seems best to you.

For those who didn't take the preceding sentence as ample reason to skip to the next section, here's the explanation: "Justification" refers to the way you line up the margins of your text. Logically (and on your toolbar), there are four possibilities:

- Line up the left margin but not the right. This is called "left justification" or, more picturesquely, "ragged right."
- Line up both the left and the right margins. This is called "full justification" but is also confusingly referred to as "justification." When someone refers to text as "justified," he means that it's fully justified. This book is fully justified.
- Line up the right margin but not the left (you guessed it— "right justification").
- Center each line.

27. You can find a useful introduction to small caps and lower-case numerals on Adobe's website, *at* http://www.adobe.com.

For the main text of a document, only left and full justification are used. The other two schemes are reserved for headings, captions and other special snatches of text.

"Don't worry" is a comforting rule for justification, but there are some qualifications. The first is the big one: The SEC believes that left-justified text is easier to read than fully justified text. You can find this conclusion in *A Plain English Handbook* put out by the SEC's Office of Investor Education and Assistance.[28] (The Handbook's views on justification are only a recommendation, but they're the recommendation of a book for which Arthur Levitt wrote the introduction. 'Nuff said?)

Don't get me wrong—I love the *Handbook*. I wish every lawyer would read and follow it. In the *Handbook's* whole length, I only found one other minor point to object to (slim pickings for a curmudgeon like me). But on this point, I think the *Handbook* went awry.

According to the *Handbook,* studies show that left justified text is easier to read because fully justified text often has uneven spacing between words. This makes seeming sense: Because each line is likely to contain a different number of letters, you can only make that right margin line up if you expand or compress the spaces between the words. (It sounds like a lot of work, but your word processing program does it automatically.) Such irregular spacing could make the text more difficult to read.

Except that it usually doesn't. If you tell your word processor to automatically hyphenate your document (and you should), the adjustments to spacing that allow the right margin to line up will seldom be obtrusive. And there is a large body of evidence that full justification is *easier* to read.

Because "studies" seem to be the rage, let's conduct our own. Go to your local Borders and start thumbing through the merchandise. You'll find that almost all books are fully justified. Now go to the magazine rack and flip some pages. You'll find a fair number of magazines that are left justified, but the majority are fully justified. The designers of these publications want them to be readable (OK, I'll make an exception for *Wired*). What do they

---

28. SECURITIES & EXCHANGE COMMISSION, A PLAIN ENGLISH HANDBOOK: HOW TO CREATE CLEAR SEC DISCLOSURE DOCUMENTS, *available at* http://www.sec.gov/news/extra/handbook.htm.

know? I can believe that fully-justified text is no more readable than left-justified text, but that it's *less* readable!? It would take a pretty good argument to convince me.

The *Handbook* gives an unconvincing example. More convincingly, it quotes (the other) Robin Williams: "There has been a great deal of research on readability . . . and it shows that those disruptive, inconsistent gaps between words inhibit the flow of reading."[29]

But the SEC is quoting Williams out of context. Her rule for justification is "Justify [i.e., fully justify] text only if the line is long enough to prevent awkward and inconsistent word spacing."[30] How long is long enough? It varies with the type size, but Williams says that for 10-point type (common in prospectuses), a mere 3.3 inches is long enough, and four inches is long enough for 12-point type.[31]

Ms. Williams' own books are fully justified. She admits to being unhappy about the uneven word spacing, but likes the look of fully justified type, "at least for some projects." (Similarly, my privets look best top-justified.) It's a trade-off, she admits.[32] The conclusion must be that if your line is long enough—and it usually is—full justification's uneven word spacing will not be a serious impediment to readability.

Hey, what happened!?

Don't worry, I've briefly switched to two columns and ragged right to show you something.

If, as I've suggested, justification isn't all that important, it might not seem to matter if you're forced to use left justification. Not always.

Documents set in columns often benefit from full justification.

Legal documents contain lots of lists. A good way to present a list (sanctioned by the *Handbook*) is in separate paragraphs set off with numbers or bullets. Here's an example:

---

29. *Id.* at 44 (citing WILLIAMS, *supra* note 20, at 46).
30. WILLIAMS, *supra* note 20, at 45.
31. *Id.* at 46.
32. *Id.*

What actor in what film said, "I just want to enter my house justified"? Was it

- Joel McCrae in *Ride the High Country,* directed by Sam Peckinpah, 1962?,
- Orson Welles in *Touch of Evil,* dir. Orson Welles, 1958? or
- Richard Barthelmess in *Only Angels Have Wings,* dir. Howard Hawks, 1939?,
- all of which have a better claim to the American Film

Institute's top 100 than some of the Oscar trash that made the list.

- Notice what's happening at the left margin of the bulleted list. The bullets line up fine, but the subsequent lines are indented ("hanging indents").
- This makes the left margin pulsate in and out. And opposite this right column, the ragged right margin of the column is swaying to and fro.

I find the erratic left-right shifting of the space between the columns distracting. Fully justifying the columns would bring some order out of the chaos, reducing the port-to-starboard roll before seasickness sets in.

So should you use full or left justification for the columns in your prospectuses? Left justification, of course! Until the SEC changes its view, there's no sense violating a "recommendation" made with such insistence. (Ms. Williams' quote, which is used as the text to demonstrate various formatting options, makes no fewer than 11 appearances in the *Handbook.*) You can handle the sway problem by not using hanging indents for bulleted lists. It's not the best solution, but you can live with it.

The problem with legislating (OK, recommending) writing and formatting standards is that, although they may improve the average product, they tend to constrict the better writers—those who know when a rule should be broken.

Take the SEC's insistence on the active voice. Some sentences work better in the passive. For example, a prize will be awarded (There's that passive again!) to anyone who can improve the following by rephrasing it in the active voice:

It is a truth universally acknowledged, that a single man in possession of a good fortune must be in want of a wife.

Everyone acknowledges that . . . ? Well, you get the point. Still, one can sympathize with the SEC. The always-use-the-active-voice rule makes sense: Prospectuses have not been written by a gang of Austens *manqué*. More like *manglé*.

But the SEC's recommendation on justification is unlikely to improve the average product. There's a lesson here. The *Handbook* erred because it briefly forgot the fundamental rule for all document design decisions: First, Look Around![33]

CENTERED TEXT

Legal documents often have centered headings and legends. I have a suspicion that the popularity of centering goes back to the early days of word processing. Suddenly it became easy to center text, but the text was still in Courier. Because there were so few ways to distinguish headings from body text (you couldn't use different size type or a different type face) centering may have recommended itself.

There's no particular reason to center headings nowadays, and centering tends to lose the strong verticals that designers— and readers—like. For myself, I find that centered text is somewhat lifeless. I tend to use it only for regulatory legends, for which embalming is appropriate.

OK, you're convinced. A couple of keystrokes, a few mouse clicks, and your document suddenly looks *great*! Now let's apply what we have learned up to this point to a fairly typical (i.e., typically egregious) bit of legal prose.

---

33. And the winner is . . . Joel McCrae in *Ride the High Country*!

AN EXERCISE BREAK

Let's apply what we have learned on the four-sentence behemoth set out in the box below. The example is taken from a credit agreement. I've indicated the four sentence breaks with circled numerals.

①(b) If as a result of any present and future taxes, assessments or governmental charges (together, "Taxes") imposed by the United States of America, or **any** political subdivision or taxing authority thereof, any Bank (or its Lending Office) shall be subject to any deduction or withholding with respect to any payment (including fees) in respect of its Loans or its Notes, the Borrower shall (i) increase the amount of such payment so that such Bank will receive a net amount (after deduction of all Taxes) equal to the amount due hereunder, (ii) pay such Taxes to the appropriate taxing authority for the account of such Bank, and (iii) as promptly as possible thereafter, send such Bank evidence showing payment thereof, together with such additional documentary evidence as such Bank may from time to time require. ②The Borrower shall indemnify any Bank for any incremental taxes, interest or penalties that may become payable as a result of any failure by the Borrower to comply with clauses (ii) or (iii) above. ③Notwithstanding the foregoing, the Borrower shall not be required to make any payment to any Bank under this subsection (b) as a result of any deduction or withholding or incremental tax, interest or penalty that is required in respect of such Bank by reason of such Bank's failure or inability to furnish any Tax Form pursuant to subsection 8.05(a) or any extension or renewal thereof, unless such failure or inability is the result of an amendment to or a change in any applicable law or regulation or in the interpretation thereof by any regulatory authority (including without limitation any change in an applicable tax treaty) that becomes effective after the date hereof. ④Each Bank will promptly notify the Borrower of any event of which it has knowledge which will entitle such Bank to compensation pursuant to this subsection.

One of the nice features of the example, for pedagogical purposes, is that it deals with taxes. The tax sections of most agreements are written—perhaps "constructed" would be a more appropriate verb—by specialists. Much the same can be said of the ERISA sections of most agreements. Most lawyers are reluctant to tamper with the substance of these sections, and in the following discussion I'll assume that the section makes legal sense.

Tax and ERISA sections are among the banes of my existence (though perhaps my existence has more banes than most). The experts who write these sections seldom deal directly with the businesspeople and feel little pressure to write clearly or to harmonize their sections with the rest of the document. In addition, their particular specialties require them to wallow in statutes, rules, regulations, orders, opinions, mandates and other governmental effluvia not noted for concision or grace.

The main problem with these sections, however, is that their perpetrators want to strut their stuff. If you know a lot about something about which most people don't give a hoot, you are likely to ignore the glazed expressions of your audience and seize the opportunity to unburden yourself of a mini-treatise. Too many tax and ERISA sections are stuffed with statutory references and other ornamentations intended to impress the audience with the extent of the specialist's learning.

Well, that felt good. As you might imagine, someone with my peculiar interests is likely to spend a fair part of every workday venting.

Returning to our example: We can improve the section by mechanically applying some of the rules in the preceding chapters to give us:

---

①(b) If as a result of ~~any present and future~~ a taxes, assessment~~s~~ or governmental charge~~s~~ (together, "Taxes") imposed by the United States of America, ~~or any~~ its political subdivisions or taxing their authorit~~iesy~~ ~~thereof~~, any Bank (or its Lending Office) ~~shall be~~ is subject to ~~any~~ deduction or withholding ~~with respect to any~~ of a payment (including fees) ~~in respect of~~ on its Loans or its Notes, the Borrower shall

(i) increase the ~~amount of such~~ payment so that ~~such~~ the Bank ~~will~~ receives a net amount (after deduction of all Taxes) equal to the amount due ~~hereunder~~,

(ii) pay ~~such~~ the Taxes to the appropriate taxing authority for the Bank's account ~~of such Bank~~, and

(iii) as promptly as possible ~~thereafter~~, send ~~such~~ the Bank evidence showing payment ~~thereof~~ of the taxes, together with ~~such~~ any additional documentary evidence ~~as such~~ the Bank ~~may from time to time~~ requires.

②The Borrower shall indemnify ~~any~~ the Bank for ~~any~~ incremental taxes, interest or penalties that ~~may~~ become payable as a result of ~~any failure by~~ the Borrower's failure to comply with clauses (ii) or (iii) above. ③Each Bank will promptly notify the Borrower of any event of which it has knowledge ~~which~~ that will entitle the Bank to compensation pursuant to this ~~sub~~section 8.05(b).

(c) Failure to Furnish Forms. ④Notwithstanding ~~the foregoing~~ section 8.05(b) above, the Borrower ~~shall~~ need not ~~be required to~~ make ~~any~~ payment to ~~any~~ Bank under ~~this~~ subsection 8.05(b) as a result of ~~any~~ deduction or withholding or incremental tax, interest or penalty that is required ~~in respect of such~~ <u>of the</u> Bank by reason of ~~such~~ <u>the</u> Bank's failure or inability to furnish ~~any~~ Tax Form pursuant to ~~sub~~section 8.05(a) or ~~any~~ extension or renewal ~~thereof~~ <u>of the tax form</u>, unless ~~such~~ <u>the</u> failure or inability is the result of an amendment to or a change in ~~any~~ applicable law or regulation or in ~~the~~ <u>its</u> interpretation ~~thereof~~ by ~~any~~ regulatory authority (including ~~without limitation~~ ~~any~~ change in an applicable tax treaty) that becomes effective after the date ~~hereof~~ <u>of this agreement</u>.

Without blackline:

(b) **Withholding taxes.** If as a result of a tax, assessment or governmental charge (together, *Taxes*) imposed by the United States of America, its political subdivisions or their taxing authorities, a Bank (or its lending office) is subject to a deduction or withholding of a payment (including fees) on its loans or its notes, the Borrower shall

(i) increase the payment so that the Bank receives a net amount (after deduction of all taxes) equal to the amount due,

(ii) pay the taxes to the appropriate taxing authority for the Bank's account, and

(iii) as promptly as possible, send the Bank evidence showing payment of the taxes, together with any additional documentary evidence the Bank requires.

The Borrower shall indemnify the Bank for incremental taxes, interest or penalties that become payable as a result of the Borrower's failure to comply with clauses (ii) or (iii) above. Each Bank will promptly notify the Borrower of any event of which it has knowledge that will entitle the Bank to compensation pursuant to this section 8.05(b).

> (c) **Failure to Furnish Forms.** Notwithstanding section 8.05(b) above, the Borrower need not make a payment to a Bank under section 8.05(b) as a result of a deduction or withholding or incremental tax, interest or penalty that is required of the Bank by reason of the Bank's failure or inability to furnish a tax form pursuant to section 8.05(a) or an extension or renewal of the tax form, *unless* the failure or inability is the result of an amendment to or a change in an applicable law or regulation or in its interpretation by a regulatory authority (including a change in an applicable tax treaty) that becomes effective after the date of this agreement.

The revised section is still something of a mess, but it is an easier read. My point was only to show the power of a few simple rules, and I resisted the temptation to make the further changes the section merits for the time being. However, now that we've seen what improvements can be made on the cheap, so to speak, let's yield to that temptation and conduct a more substantial rewrite:

> (b) **Withholding taxes.** If ~~as a result of~~ a tax, assessment or governmental charge (together, *taxes*) imposed by the United States ~~of America~~, its political subdivisions or their taxing authorities, <u>subjects</u> a Bank (or its lending office) ~~is subject~~ to a deduction or withholding of a payment (including fees) on its loans or its notes, the Borrower shall
> (iv) increase the payment so that the Bank receives a net amount (after deduction of all taxes) equal to the amount due,
> (v) pay the taxes ~~to the appropriate taxing authority~~ for the Bank's account, and
> (vi) ~~as~~ promptly ~~as possible~~, send the Bank <u>any</u> <u>documentary</u> evidence ~~showing~~ <u>of</u> payment of the taxes<u>,</u> ~~together with any additional documentary evidence~~ the Bank requires.

The Borrower shall indemnify the Bank for incremental taxes, interest or penalties ~~that become payable as a result of~~ caused by the Borrower's failure to comply with clauses (ii) or (iii) above. Each Bank will promptly notify the Borrower of any event ~~of which~~ it ~~has knowledge that~~ knows will entitle it ~~the Bank~~ to compensation ~~pursuant to~~ under this section 8.05(b).

(c) **Failure to furnish forms.** Notwithstanding section 8.05(b) above, the Borrower need not ~~make a payment to~~ pay a Bank under subsection 8.05(b) ~~as a result of~~ for a deduction or withholding or incremental tax, interest or penalty that is ~~required of the Bank by reason of~~ caused by the Bank's failure ~~or inability~~ to furnish a tax form pursuant to section 8.05(a) or an extension or renewal of the tax form, unless the failure ~~or inability is the~~ results from ~~of an amendment to or~~ a change in ~~an applicable~~ the law, treaty or regulation or in its interpretation by a regulatory authority ~~(including a change in an applicable tax treaty)~~ that becomes effective after the date of this agreement.

Without blackline:

(b) **Withholding taxes.** If a tax, assessment or governmental charge (together, *taxes*) imposed by the United States, its political subdivisions or their taxing authorities subjects a Bank (or its lending office) to a deduction or withholding of a payment (including fees) on its loans or notes, the Borrower shall

(i) increase the payment so that the Bank receives a net amount (after deduction of all taxes) equal to the amount due,

(ii) pay the taxes for the Bank's account, and

(iii) promptly send the Bank any documentary evidence of payment of the taxes the Bank requires.

The Borrower shall indemnify the Bank for incremental taxes, interest or penalties caused by the Borrower's failure to comply with clauses (ii) or (iii) above. Each Bank will promptly notify the Borrower of any event it knows will entitle it to compensation under this section 8.05(b).

(c) **Failure to furnish forms.** Notwithstanding section 8.05(b) above, the Borrower need not pay a Bank under subsection 8.05(b) for a deduction or withholding or incremental tax, interest or penalty that is caused by the Bank's failure to furnish a tax form pursuant to section 8.05(a) or an extension or renewal of the tax form *unless* the failure results from a change in a law, treaty or regulation, or in its interpretation by a regulatory authority, that becomes effective after the date of this agreement.

Still not Shakespeare, but I was inhibited by a lack of knowledge of the tax laws. For example, do you really need to refer to an extension or renewal of the tax form? I could find out, but my aim here is not to teach tax law. Despite these limitations, the final version is much easier to read than the original, if only because a full quarter of the words have disappeared.

To this point, I've dealt with issues that apply to legal documents generally. The rest of this book will deal first with agreements, then with other types of documents, beginning with the securities prospectus.

PARTICULAR DOCUMENTS

AGREEMENTS

Every story is supposed to have a beginning, a middle and an end. Legal documents, especially agreements, have a story to tell; however, in a well-wrought agreement, the action does not rise to a climax with a dénouement near the end. Good agreements are constructed like news stories—the most important stuff is at the beginning, and the least important stuff is at the end.

Most important to what end? To the understanding of the business bargain, of course. The agreement will have lots of legal and accounting tidbits, but the first appetite to be satisfied is the businessperson's. She must see the document as the statement of her deal, not as a legal nicety akin to an incumbency certificate.

Structuring an agreement means arranging an orderly flow of subject matter from most important to least important. So what should go first? In most agreements, a table of contents.

The Table of Contents

An agreement is made of parts usually called *sections*. Some agreements refer to parts of sections as sub-sections and to groups of sections as articles, but I'll use "section" as a blanket term for any contiguous and related group of paragraphs. In my usage, a single section can itself be made up of smaller sections.

Every moderately lengthy section that deals with a single subject should have a title. This section, for example, is titled "the table of contents," and is part of a larger section called "Agreements."

Titling sections serves at least three purposes: First, on the purely visual level, section titles break up the flow of text. This provides a welcome relief for the eye and the mind. A section title should mark a point where the subject matter shifts, if only slightly, thus marking an appropriate place to take a break of seconds or days.

Second, a section title provides a convenient means of cross-reference. A sentence in a credit agreement might, for example, make the principal amount of each loan payable on a certain date, "subject to section 7.1, 'action on event of default'," which section provides the lender with the right to bring forward the maturity date of the loans under certain circumstances. If you refer to the section title, the reader can easily locate the section and is likely to understand why the payment is subject to section 7.1.

The most important function of section titles, however, is to make the document comprehensible. This is accomplished by listing, in order, the section titles in outline form at the front of the document in a table of contents.

Think about the last time you wandered around the nonfiction section of a bookstore. When you took a book off the shelf, very likely the first thing you looked at was the table of contents. The table probably gave you more information about the book than any other similar sized part of the book.

It's the same with legal documents. Properly constructed, the table of contents serves as an outline of the document. An outline is a powerful engine for organizing information; yet, it is the rare document that titles and arranges its sections to tell a coherent story.

The current inadequacy of the table of contents is probably a hangover from the days when they had to be manually typed for each new draft. If a document is properly set up (not an arduous task), modern word processing programs will automatically generate a new table of contents each time the document is printed, and today's programs can do a great deal more.

In my word processing program, for example, you can shift almost instantaneously from the document to an outline view of the document. The outline is, in essence, the table of contents (i.e., the section titles) without the page numbers. In outline mode, you can both edit the headings and change their order.

And when you move the headings, *the text under the headings goes along.* You can also change the level of the section titles. For example, if you're looking at two consecutive section titles, "prepayment" and "maturity," you might decide to make the prepayment section a subsection of the maturity section. A couple mouse clicks and it's done.

The fundamental principle of toxicology is that it's possible to have too much of almost any good thing. The same can be said of a table of contents that runs on page after page. This may be unavoidable for the table of contents of the Uniform Commercial Code, but it's seldom necessary for an agreement or prospectus. I don't know how to tell you where to draw the line, so for now I'll just caution you that a table of contents can be too long as well as too short. In my own documents, I have occasionally had three or more levels of section titles but included only the top two in the table of contents. (This trick is duck soup for a word processing program.)

The moral of the story is that section titles should work as parts of a table of contents that provides an organized overview—informative but not exhausting—of the agreement.

ENTRANCES AND EXITS

The Title. Most of the agreements I encounter announce themselves with a long title like:

> **Revolving Credit Agreement** dated as of April 1, 2000 among Acme Widget Corp. (the "Borrower"), the Lenders named herein, First National Bank of Mugwump, as Managing Agent, and Gargantua Bank, N.A., as Administrative Agent (the "Administrative Agent")

It's not usually called a "title," but I don't know what else to call it. It comes at the beginning and it's not a sentence—that would require a verb. Perhaps we're meant to understand that this title is preceded by a silent "The following is a," but I'll continue to refer to it as the title of the agreement.

What I call a title is often preceded by something that everyone would call a title—in my example it might consist of the words "revolving credit agreement" in full caps and centered.

The title, or titles, usually precede a statement that "The parties agree as follows:," which marks the beginning of the body of the agreement—the covenants, representations, conditions and other terms of the standard contemporary written contract. Sandwiched between the title and the body of the agreement a reader may find a recital of facts that may help him understand the agreement's background. At the end of the agreement come the signatures of the parties.[34]

These contractual elements are so standard that it may surprise many lawyers that you can do them differently. For the past few years, I have begun my agreements like this:[35]

Revolving Credit Agreement
April 1, 2000
PARTIES
- Acme Widget Corp. (the *Borrower*)
- the *Lenders* named below
- **First National Bank of Mugwump,** as *Managing Agent*
- **Gargantua Bank, N.A.,** as *Administrative Agent*
BACKGROUND
[recitals]
AGREEMENT
[terms of the agreement]

There's nothing really *wrong* with the standard title, but I think my presentation is a bit easier to follow. Each of the elements of the title—the name of the agreement, the date and the parties are listed separately and the recitals and the agreement are also broken out. Now that we've broken the elements out, let's discuss them individually.

---

34. The signatures may be followed by schedules and exhibits, which I discuss in "Schedules and Exhibits" at 96.

35. Much of the following format was suggested to me by Robert S. Schwartz of Columbus, Ohio.

There's not a whole lot to say about the title. It should usually contain the word "agreement" so that people will instantly
know that they are looking at a document intended to be legally
binding. And it's nice if you can say a little bit more to get readers oriented, but not too much. "Revolving credit agreement" fills
these requirements nicely.

The Date. I can say a lot more about the date. A date could
be read as either specifying the date the agreement is entered into
or the date it is to be effective. Usually, but not always, the signing date and the effective date are the same. Most lawyers date
agreements "as of " a date to alert readers that the date of the
agreement is not necessarily the date it was signed.

One of the smartest lawyers I know once told me that when
he was fresh out of law school, he somehow was briefly left in
charge of one side of an all-night drafting session. While in
charge, he objected to dating a document "as of " a certain date (a
practice with which he had no familiarity) because it smacked of
hanky-panky. (Older readers may recall that about that time President Nixon's lawyer got in some well-publicized trouble for
backdating a deed of gift to evidence a charitable contribution on
the President's tax return.) The senior partner on the other side,
after trying in vain to explain to my friend that everybody dated
documents "as of " and that the practice was entirely innocent,
stalked off and locked himself in a conference room for an hour
to cool off, by which time my friend's superiors had returned to
set matters straight.

The view that you have to date a document "as of " unless it
is actually signed on the particular date is one of those cases of a
practice gestating into a myth. The parties should date the document the date that they intend it to become legally binding: Acts
done before that date are not covered by the agreement (except
by special provision), acts done after are covered (again, except
by special provision). You don't need "as of " to make that point.

Whether you prefer to retain "as of " or drop it, as I do, you
should still ask about the appropriateness of backdating a document. If the date only affects the rights and obligations of the parties, there can be no harm to it. If the date may affect others'

rights and obligations, I would be reluctant to backdate the agreement beyond the date that the parties had reached a binding legal agreement, although this might be a date well before a definitive document was executed. (Note that minutes of a board meeting are dated the date, not "as of" the date, of the board meeting, even though the minutes may be finalized and signed days or months later.)

What about "foredating," i.e., dating a document several days or weeks after signing? I'd always regarded this as unproblematic until I encountered a lawyer who refused to foredate documents because he thought foredating would give a party the power to revoke the agreement during the interval between the document's signing and its date. (He continued to worry regardless of whether the document was dated "as of.") I can't see the argument. If a foredated agreement isn't binding, it must at least constitute an offer by each signatory, which would make the signatures of the other parties an acceptance. An offer can't be revoked once it has been accepted.

One final point on dating: I've never understood why the date of a document has to be preceded by the word "dated." If you've positioned the date in the proper place—adjacent to either the title at the beginning or the signatures at the end—there can be no doubt that a date standing alone is the date of the document. And if you can conceive of such a doubt, then it's just as easy to conceive a doubt as to what the word "dated" refers to; is it the document that is "dated April 1, 2000," or is it something else?

List of Parties. There is little to be said here about the list of parties. I've already expounded upon the virtues of bulleted lists.[36] Clearly, it's easier to see who the characters are if they are presented, with their stage names, in a bulleted list.

Recitals. A lot could be written about recitals, but not by me. Some agreements benefit from them, some do not. For example, I would normally think that a revolving credit agreement does not require recitals. For agreements that are less straightforward, I find recitals useful. They should be written so that they set the

---

36. *See* "Untangling the Legal Sentence—Sentences That Run Too Long" at 17.

stage for an understanding of the agreement but should not run on to tedious length. I won't pretend it's easy.

Two small points about recitals I will address: First, there's no reason to begin each sentence of the recital with a "Whereas." If you label the recitals section adequately, readers will know they are reading recitals without the "whereas" tag. "Whereas" is another bit of legal mummery that is best dispensed with.

The second point is that most nonlawyers don't use the word "recital" in the legal sense, so I usually caption the recitals section as "Background."

Following the recitals, the real work of the agreement begins. Most agreements mark this point with the words "the parties agree as follows." Frankly, I find this a bit stodgy. People will understand that what follows is the real agreement if you just caption it "agreement."[37]

We can now swoop to the end of the agreement. Immediately preceding the signatures you may find the impressive phrase "In Witness Whereof, the parties have executed this agreement on the date set forth at the beginning hereof." Most agreements now manage without this phrase, which is usually called a "testimonium." The origins of the testimonium are obscure, but I think we can agree that it's surplusage to be consigned to the flames.

This brings us to the signatures. The UCC, discussing negotiable instruments gives "P[rincipal], by A[gent], Treasurer" as an example of a signature that "unambiguously shows that it is made on behalf of an identified represented person." In such a case, the represented person, P, would be liable on the instrument, but not the representative, A.[38] The UCC rules for liability on instruments are generally followed for liability on other documents.

For a corporation, the signature is usually written:

Acme Widget Corp.

By [signature]
President

---

37. In "Agreements—Interpreting Section Titles" at 89, I caution against the standard boilerplate provision that section titles and captions are not part of the agreement.

38. U.C.C. § 3-402(b) (1990) and official cmt. 2.

Such a signature binds Acme on the document but not its representative, in this case its president.

It has on occasion troubled me that the name of the corporation is separated from its representative. I've attempted to remedy this with signature blocks that look like:

Acme Widget Corp.

By [signature]
President

or even

Acme Widget Corp.

By [signature]
President

but it's a lot of work, so I usually settle for the signature block style everyone else uses.

THE DEFINITIONAL TANGLE

After the recitals, the next major piece of a legal document a reader will commonly encounter is a definition section. Non-lawyers regard the definition section as a necessary but bloated evil. Obviously, definitions are essential. Without them, many sentences that are already too long for easy comprehension would run to impossible lengths. Because the same defined terms are used repeatedly, a definition section at the front of the document where defined terms are set out alphabetically makes a good deal of sense—or used to.

There are problems with the definition section as currently designed. A reader must constantly turn from the substantive sections back to the definition section. This side trip can become an odyssey if the reader discovers that the definition itself contains defined terms, which may themselves be defined in terms of defined terms, and so on. Eventually the reader will arrive at definitions that contain no defined terms. At that point, the reader must retrace his steps, building up toward the term that originally sent him to the definition section.

The alternative to these excursions is for the reader to read the definition section carefully enough to understand the defined terms before turning to the rest of the document. Many readers attempt this, if only from the natural tendency to read the document in the order presented. But this method has its own pitfalls. Defined terms are difficult to understand if they are not immediately used, yet the reader must usually wait many pages before he can see how the defined term functions in the document.

Just as serious is the problem of learning the defined terms in alphabetical order. Aside from the alphabet itself, I can think of no subject that is best taught in alphabetical order. The best way to learn anything is to start with simple concepts and build toward more complex ones, but this logical order has no relation to alphabetical order.

The easiest way to understand a defined term is to have it defined "on site," i.e., in the context where it is used, with more complex terms built up from simpler ones. However, if the defined term is used again later on, the reader may have to search back through the document to find the definition.

One way to have the advantages of "on site" definitions and a definition section is to have the defined term in the definition section refer to the section where the "on site" definition appears (e.g., "consolidated adjusted tangible net worth" has the meaning specified in Section 4.6(b)"). This is done in many documents, but in a fragmentary manner. The key to improving the definition section is to systematically exploit this technique.

Defined terms form a continuum of comprehensibility, from those that are understood by the intended readers without reference to the document (e.g., "capital lease," "ERISA," "prime rate") to those that have no meaning apart from the document (e.g., "crossover date," "redistribution payment"). Readers will differ with respect to the ordering, but a rough ordering can usually be made.

Once you realize that not all defined terms are the same, you have a tool for unraveling the definitional tangle. The first step is to define those terms that lie on the "must be defined" end of the continuum on-site in a logical order. Those terms that are relatively familiar can be left in the definition section; defining them on-site will only clutter up the substantive provisions of the document.

Next, you should create an index of defined terms, placed immediately after the table of contents or, in a securities prospectus, at the end of the document. If each defined term is appropriately coded, your word processor will assemble the definition index automatically. The index will give the page number of each definition, including the defined terms in the definition section. For a number of reasons, page references in a definition index are easier to use than section references in a definition section. First, the definition index only takes up a page or two, so the reference can be found faster. Second, a page reference is easier to use than a section reference because the reader knows about where the page is (e.g., page 33 is a bit more than one-third of the way through a 90 page document) and because every page has a page number.

You should take care that terms defined on-site are easy to find on the page. The standard method—enclosing the defined term in quotation marks—is inadequate. A better solution, possible with modern printers, is to print defined terms in *italics* or ***bold italics***.

You should now delete from the definition section all references to terms that are defined on-site. With a definition index, these references become unnecessary. Finally, since the only terms remaining in the definition section are those that are generally understandable without resort to the definitions, you should move the definition section to the back of the document. A reader won't need these definitions to get into the agreement, so putting the definition section first will only delay him.

Putting First Things First

So, the definition section should be last. But what should be first? Lawyers have conventions for ordering long documents, and following those conventions makes navigation easier for other lawyers. But nonlawyers also read these documents. Could a different order make our documents less confusing?

The current conventions get many matters back-to-front. Points that are unimportant to the business deal are thrust forward while critical issues bring up the rear. Unraveling the document requires learning a form of legal Hebrew.

You should begin the document with the most important part of the document—the description of the deal. Unfortunately, it's possible to start at the back end of the deal description.

An agreement should begin with those points most important to the nonlegal participants and end with those points that are least important. In the deal description, the most important point is almost always money—how much is being paid or lent, what fees are owed, what interest rate is being charged. An agreement starts most happily when the first statement (after introduction of the *dramatis personae*) is something on the order of "Microdigidiagnostics, Inc. will sell its brain replacement business to Advanced Quackery Systems Inc. for 16 gazillion dollars." That's putting first things first. We can then move on to the details of what is included in the brain replacement business and how the gazillions are to be paid.

Revolving credit agreements traditionally follow their tedious definition section with a section on the loans. The loan section is usually structured around the chronology of a loan—that is, it starts with how you borrow, moves on to the interest on the borrowing and wraps up with repayment mechanics. Chronology is a useful structuring device, but here it manages to sandwich the money terms between those fascinating sections on borrowing and repayment notices. I generally draft revolving credit agreements with separate sections for loan *terms,* by which I mean money matters, and loan *procedures,* which includes all the mechanics. Readers may guess which section goes first.

In many agreements, the deal description is followed by the four sisters of documentation—sections for representations and warranties, conditions, covenants (sometimes divided into affirmative and negative covenants) and defaults. What is the proper order for these sections? And what is the proper order for the material within these sections?

One guide for ordering the four sisters is a term sheet for the deal, and the best term sheet is likely to be an early draft that lacks the clutter of later legal interventions. An early term sheet, if you are lucky enough to have one, will give the best insight into the businesspeople's order of priorities. The businesspeople's order isn't necessarily the best order, but it is an order that deserves the drafter's respect.

Many legal documents order the four sisters chronologically: Representations and warranties (which state how things are at closing) come first, followed by the conditions to closing (one of which will be the accuracy of the reps and warranties). Then come covenants, which govern the parties' conduct after closing. Finally, default, which describes the least desirable final act.

This order is not always appropriate. For example, conditions to closing may be unimportant in a contract for the ongoing provision of services but critically important in an agreement for acquisition financing. Similarly, covenants may be critical to a revolving credit agreement but unimportant in a sale of assets (where the representations are likely to be key).

I once drafted a collateral administration agreement under which a bank would be custodian for collateral pledged to several lenders. For the lenders, the value of the collateral and how and when they could reach it were the core of the agreement. So I placed the borrower's covenant to maintain the value of the pledged collateral and the default and liquidation provisions immediately after the description of the collateral and the grant of the security interest. The mechanical procedures for synchronizing collateral deposits and releases with loan disbursements and repayments came after. Covenants by each party regarding compliance with rules governing the pledge of margin stock, which were of special concern to the custodian and the lenders, went into a separate section labeled "margin stock issues." The representations and warranties, which were thin, were placed well back. I'm not sure it was the best ordering, but at least it got some thought.

It is the order within the sisters, however, that best evidences the lawyer's penchant for reverse locomotion. Almost every representation and warranty section starts with a shadow legal opinion—representations as to due incorporation, valid existence, enforceability and so forth. In a sense, these representations are basic, but in another sense they are trivial. They are representations that had better be true for the deal to work, but in much the sense that the law of gravity had better be true. No businesspeople ever discuss them, so they are fit material for the back of the book.

The traditional order of covenants is almost as bad. The covenant section is often divided into "affirmative" and "negative" covenants. Even if that terminology is not used, "do" covenants tend to precede "don't" covenants. This may seem a commendable attempt to accentuate the positive, but it also buries the businesspeople's fundamental concerns more deeply in the document. In a credit agreement, for example, the first covenant usually deals with such fascinating affirmative matters as the provision of reports. Negative covenants may begin with general prohibitions of liens, debt, guaranties and mergers. Way back at the end come the life or death nonlegal issues, such as the financial tests the borrower must meet. By any logic, these covenants should come first, followed by the other negative covenants and then the affirmative covenants.

The upside-down construction of many agreements has a simple, and preventable, cause: The drafter started with a venerable form and then modified it to fit the particular transaction. There is an all-too-natural tendency to stick the unique bits of the agreement at the end of a section. But the unique bits are the bits the businesspeople focused on; these hard-bargained terms should not be tucked in at the end for the sake of preserving the appearance of a form agreement.

INTERPRETING SECTION TITLES

Many agreements and other legal documents that use section titles extensively include something like the following zinger in the back:

> Article and section headings and the table of contents of this agreement are for convenience of reference only, are

not part of this agreement and are not to be taken into consideration in interpreting this agreement.

I'll refer to this bit of boilerplate as the "I'm-not-here" clause.

There's a scene in Otto Preminger's *Anatomy of a Murder* where Joseph Welsch, playing the judge in a murder trial, tells the jury to ignore a particularly argumentative question by defense counsel Jimmy Stewart. The defendant, Ben Gazzara, asks, "How can they ignore what they just heard?" "They can't," replies Stewart.

Similarly, we can ask how someone who reads a section title can ignore it in interpreting the section, especially when most of us will admit that the main virtue of chapter and section titling is to help us find our way into the text.

These reflections set the stage for an interesting debate about section titling in the Uniform Commercial Code (UCC to its friends). Section 1-109 of the UCC, as enacted in 34 states, provides that "section captions are part of this Act." (I'll call this the "I'm-here" clause.) However, sixteen other states have omitted the I'm-here clause or actively negated it.[39]

Some proponents of dropping the I'm-here clause wish only to increase the use of titling, retaining section titles and adding titles to at least some subsections and paragraphs, which are not now titled anywhere in the UCC. They hope that drafters will use more titles if they feel that they aren't making too big a commitment.

But with or without I'm-here or I'm-not-here clauses, people are going to rely on section titles. Consider the following example of how a section title can affect the interpretation of a statutory provision:

New York's UCC used to include the following nonuniform provision:

No financing statement, security agreement, or other related statement shall be accepted for filing unless it is

---

39. Louis F. Del Duca, Vincent C. DeLiberato, Jr., David L. Hostetter, Steven O. Weise, *Revisiting the Application of Plain English in Revising the UCC—Current Practice among the 50 States on Use of Captions in Legislation,* 30 UCC L.J. 167 (Fall 1997).

typed or printed in black ink and in the determination of the filing officer it can be legibly read, scanned, interpreted or reproduced by the technology employed by the department of state.

Here's some background to help you appreciate the potential difficulties in interpreting the preceding "black ink" provision: UCC section 9-402, which was titled (in part) "formal requisites of financing statement," stated that a financing statement was *sufficient* if it fulfilled certain conditions. These conditions did not include ink color but did include giving the name of the debtor and the name and address of the secured party. The first paragraph of section 9-403, which was titled (in part) "what constitutes filing; . . . duties of filing officer," stated that "presentation for filing of a financing statement and tender of the filing or processing fee or acceptance of the statement by the filing officer constitutes *filing* under [Article 9]" (my emphasis).

So, if you presented a blue-ink financing statement with a filing fee to a New York filing officer, had you *filed* even if the officer properly refused the filing? And if a bleary-eyed filing officer mistakenly accepted it, was the financing statement *sufficient?*

Argument 1: The black-ink provision really spoke to the duties of the filing officer because it said that a financing statement "shall [not] be accepted for filing." If the filing officer (rightly) refused to accept the blue-ink financing statement, it was not filed despite section 9-403(a)'s seemingly categorical statement that it was filed.

Argument 2: The provision was directed at sufficiency, not filing, because it required black ink so that the financing statement could be legibly reproduced. It would be ludicrous to hold that an illegible filed financing statement is sufficient. Moreover, the categorical nature of section 9-403(a) required that, even if the filing officer refused a blue-ink financing statement, it would still be *filed.*

So, was a refused blue-ink financing statement filed but not sufficient (Argument 2) or was it simply not filed (Argument 1)? And was a blue-ink financing statement accepted in error sufficient (Argument 1) or not (Argument 2)?

Silly me, did I forget to tell you that the black-ink provision was 9-403(10), which was part of the section titled (in part) "what constitutes filing; . . . duties of filing officer"? In this company, it seems obvious that black ink had nothing to do with the sufficiency of the statement (which was discussed in section 9-402, "formal requisites of financing statement; . . .") and that it qualified the general principle that mere presentation of a blue-ink financing statement with a fee constituted filing. (As a policy matter, I'm not sure this is the best outcome; there seem to be no decisions interpreting the black-ink provision.)

It could be that my interpretation is right, but that it follows from the *subject matter* of the section, not its *title*. Perhaps, but I tend to think that the section title was part of the mechanism by which the subject got to be grouped and that the New York legislature plunked the black-ink requirement down (in 1990) at the end of section 9-403 because they understood from the title that section 9-403 was about filing, not sufficiency.

Thus, it appears that, in some cases, section titling can help us understand the meaning of a provision. How often does this happen? I don't know. I can tell you, however, that it took me less than 10 minutes of flipping through the UCC to find this example. (Because the result conformed to my own views, I decided not to press my luck by looking for another.)

The disdain for section titles that leads drafters to assign them second-class citizenship may stem from a fear that little attention is likely to be paid to the drafting of section titles. Clearly, you don't want a carelessly worded title to override the carefully worded text of the section. Fair enough, but the proper response is for more attention to be paid to the titles. People (including New York legislators) rely on section titles; it makes sense to draft them carefully, and it's not all that difficult.

A deeper reason for the failure to countenance titles as part of the document is the strong, if inchoate, belief that each sentence in a legal document should hold its meaning independently of its fellows. When it comes to interpretation, each sentence should be able to stand up on its own 27 clauses and forthrightly declaim "We don't need no stinkin' titles!"

This argument is just another version of the "sentences-as-the-unit-of-truth" fallacy that I dispatched earlier.[40] We don't have to unlimber that heavy artillery to deal with this mouse, however. I'll cut the argument short with the following leading questions: Do the official comments to the UCC amplify the meaning of the statute or are they just Cliff Notes for the legal *illiterati?*

My own experience with statute drafting is limited to a two-day drafting session of the then-gestating revised article 8 of the UCC. I was not surprised to find that the drafters often used the UCC's official comments to clarify the intention of the black letter text. Hey, the comments were always a big help to me! (Interestingly, neither the text of the UCC nor the official comments say anything about the proper relation of the one to the other.)[41] If a sentence in the commentary (or the legislative history) can help you understand a sentence in the statute, why deny that a section title can confer a comparable benefice?

I don't include an I'm-not-here clause in documents I draft because I think it's silly to tell the parties not to do something that is sensible and, in any case, well-nigh irresistible. But if a court were to take the clause seriously, I think it would be much more likely to apply the clause in favor of a nondrafting party than the drafting party. There's not much firepower in an I'm-not-here clause, but what there is, is likely to be targeted at the drafter's foot.

To Number or Not To Number

Legal documents usually identify each section with a number and/or letter, and lawyers usually cross-reference other sections by their number/letter. For example, the sentence in the credit agreement that I used as an example in the preceding paragraph might have said that the principal amount of each loan was payable on a certain date, "subject to section 6(b)." The problem

---

40. *See* "Untangling the Legal Sentence—Sentences and Truth" at 42.
41. For a discussion of the relation, *see* Kenneth C. Kettering, *Repledge Deconstructed,* 61 U. Pitt. L. Rev. 45, 230–235 (Fall 1999).

with these numerical cross-references is that they are opaque to the reader, who must flip to section 6(b) or to the table of contents to understand what the maturity date is subject to. If you have to have section numbering, it's more helpful to say "subject to section 6(b), 'action on event of default'."

Section numbering is nearly universal in legal documents, but is seldom necessary. I tend to regard it as clutter and have dropped it for shorter documents. I am thinking about dropping it for longer ones as well. (This book, for example, seems to work just as well without chapter or section numbers.) If I have to cross-reference, I do it by section title alone if possible. I will, however, use section numbering for bits of the document that must be cross-referenced but are too small to justify a separate section title.

There's another problem with section numbering, especially the numbering found in statutes and regulations. It is convenient to be able to cross-reference relatively brief sections of a statute or regulation, so the section numbering tends to go down many levels, with no realistic possibility of providing titles for such small bits. A regulation thus might provide a cross-reference to, for example, "section 33.1(b)(ii)(F)(4)." Such a cross-reference is, of course, difficult to understand. It may also be nearly impossible to find.

When such long strings of numbers and letters are used, the usual practice is to number the particular section solely as "(4)." You then look up the page to find the next lettered section, which will not be identified as "33.1(b)(ii)(F)," but simply as "(F)." Finding the section can be a protracted process. You start at "33.1," scan down the page or pages to find the "(b)," continue to the "(ii)," press on to the "(F)," and finally stagger to the "(4)." Or maybe not. The numbers and letters tend to be small and densely packed, and it's not unusual to miss a key guide-post. Before you know it, you are, all unawares, in 33.1(b)(*iii*), not (ii), looking for "(F)," which, if you're unlucky, will exist to point you on to the wrong "(4)." It's happened to me and I'll bet it's happened to you.

Three solutions suggest themselves. The most natural would be to include a header or footer on each page that contains the full section number of the first full section on the page; if one page says "33.1(b)(i)(C)(2)" while the next reads "33.1(b)(iii)(A)(2)," then you know you've got the varmint cornered. This solution may be a bit difficult with current word-processing programs. My own word processor will gladly print the first section's title or number as a header, but I don't know how to print the entire number in the header and only the truncated number in the text. I imagine it's doable, but it may prove difficult for most of us.

A second solution might be to number each section in full—"33.1(b)(ii)(F)(4)" rather than "(4)." But it's not much of a solution. The visual clutter of having all those letters and numbers every few lines would probably render the document about as readable as a hieroglyph.

A third solution seems more promising, although I've never seen it done: Give the full number for each section, but place it in a separate column on the left. This solves several problems simultaneously. Every section is numbered in full, and if there is enough distance between the section number and the section, and the section numbering is done in modestly-sized type, the visual distractions of the section numbering will be substantially reduced. Placing the numbers in a second column may also encourage the use of shorter lines for the text and discourage the elaborate indenting that causes text to snake its way down the page.

Finally, as I noted at the beginning of this chapter, I tend to refer to any contiguous group of paragraphs as a "section." This has two smallish consequences: First, because there is no longer a need to distinguish sections from articles, subsections or paragraphs, there is also no need to title a section "Section 4: Covenants"; "4 Covenants" does the job nicely. Second, because a section can itself contain other sections, I have found it useful to add the following provision to the "usages" section[42] at the back of my agreements:

> References to numbered sections in this agreement also refer to all included sections. For example, references to section 6 also refer to sections 6.1, 6.1(a), etc.

---

42. Usage sections are discussed in "Untangling the Legal Sentence—Sentences That Do Too Much" at 20.

SCHEDULES AND EXHIBITS

These days, even a short commercial agreement may be swollen to telephone book dimensions by the addition of numerous and lengthy schedules and exhibits. Drafters, unfortunately, give little thought to the difficulties a reader faces in finding a particular schedule or exhibit in the throng.

Consider: You are looking for the Honorable Frederick Threepwood's employment agreement, which is the eighth of the 22 exhibits that follow the main agreement's nine schedules. The table of contents does not give you a page number for the exhibit because, as is typical in these matters, each schedule and exhibit has its own pagination. With no better guide, you take a chance and open the document to a random page about three-fourths of the way toward the end. It's page 15, but page 15 of what? You backtrack to page one of whatever-it-is and—Hoorah! Page one discloses that you have opened the document to exhibit 12. The preceding page is number 5, presumably page 5 of exhibit 11. You move forward five pages to page one of . . . exhibit 3?!? Ah, you say, it's exhibit 3 *to exhibit 11.* Or was exhibit 12 merely exhibit 12 to some other exhibit? No, that can't be because then the preceding document would be exhibit 11 to that other exhibit or schedule. Unless, of course, the exhibits to the exhibits have their own exhibits, a terrifying although unlikely possibility. Anyway, you push on and in mere minutes are at page one of the Threepwood agreement. You leave a PostIt to mark the spot because you never want to go through that again.

How can you spare your readers such exertions? For one thing, you can subject all the schedules and exhibits to a single scheme of pagination. If the schedules and exhibits are all created on the same word processor, which happens often enough, you can give the main agreement and all the schedules and exhibits the same pagination. The table of contents will then give the page number of each schedule and exhibit. A quick look at the table of contents will tell your reader that the Threepwood agreement begins on page 1,462.

But what about those exhibits—let's call them *mavericks*— that are not generated on your word processor? Well, if the maverick is not too long, you can preserve the single system of pagination by inserting blank numbered pages at the appropriate point in the document and photocopying the exhibit onto the blank pages. Still, at some point the number and length of the mavericks may make photocopying on to blank pages too complicated (although I notice that both the ABA and Practising Law Institute provide uniform pagination for their course materials).

If you can't or won't provide uniform pagination, then you can at least provide some other guides for your readers. The (second) best course is to mark each schedule and exhibit with those nice plastic pages with numbered or lettered tabs that are sold in stationery stores. They're more informative than the colored pages that are often inserted between the various schedules and exhibits.

There is one drawback to using tabbed dividers: Because the tabs are numbered starting at 1 or lettered beginning at A, it's hard to use a variant numbering or lettering scheme. In particular, this will prevent you from numbering schedules or exhibits with the section number of the agreement in which the schedule or exhibit is referenced. I like that kind of cross-referencing, but will gladly trade it for a better way to locate schedules and exhibits.

If you're going to maintain a distinction between schedules and exhibits, it's best to number schedules but use letters for exhibits, or vice-versa. But what *is* the distinction between a schedule and an exhibit? An *exhibit,* to my way of thinking, is a stand-alone document that is relevant to, but not properly part of, the main agreement. For example, the Threepwood agreement is an independent document, even though it may be tied in some way to the main agreement. Exhibits are often tacked on for the reader's convenience—a comforting thought as you lug those extra pounds of convenience to and from the office.

A *schedule,* in contrast, contains information that is properly part of the main agreement but that, for reasons discussed below, has been moved to the back. An example might be a list of notice addresses for the 60 lenders under a syndicated revolving credit agreement. The main agreement may call for notices to be sent to lenders at their notice addresses, but a lender reading the agreement will pay little attention to any address but its own. Best to move the addresses to a schedule where they will not distract from more serious matters.

Another reason for using a schedule is that the tone of the schedule may be allowed to differ from the tone of the main agreement. In "Untangling the Legal Sentence—When Once Is Too Much" at 30, I described a schedule of "haircuts" for pledged securities. The information had a high interest-to-volume ratio, but I nevertheless put it in a schedule because I was reluctant (for reasons I described) to change the businesspeople's description of the securities. For similar reasons, important technical data may be in a schedule rather than the main agreement.

Another traditional use of the schedule is for "exception" information. For example, the agreement may state that the borrower will not permit any liens on its assets "except as stated on schedule *x*." This is an acceptable practice because the scheduled liens have usually already been placed on the assets. The record of historical liens may be important from a due diligence standpoint, but for purposes of negotiating the agreement, what's done is done (well, usually).

Schedules often contain tabular information, but information shouldn't be consigned to a schedule just because it's in the form of a table. I've seen a table of the lenders' interest rates and commitment fees placed in a schedule. That's the kind of information that should go well forward in the agreement rather than far back in a schedule.

Schedules and exhibits need to be linked to the main agreement by something more substantial than a staple. Normally, this is unproblematic: A statement in the agreement that "this agreement will not become effective until an employment agreement between the Hon. Frederick Threepwood and the Perfecto Zizzbaum Motion Picture Company in substantially the form of exhibit 8 is executed and delivered" does the job nicely. Lately, however, I've noticed that many drafters use a more suspicious device for linking exhibits and schedules to the main agreement: incorporation by reference.

Incorporation by reference is respectable when properly used. The SEC permits incorporation by reference so that material filed on one form need not be repeated in another. And the Freedom of Information Act provides that readily available materials may be deemed to be published in the Federal Register if appropriately incorporated by reference.[43]

In those cases, incorporation by reference has clearly understood purposes and effects. But what is the purpose or effect of a provision that "exhibit 8 [the Hon. Freddie's employment agreement] is incorporated herein by reference"? Surely not to incorporate the rights and obligations of the Threepwood-Zizzbaum agreement; those rights and obligations run to different parties. Nor would anyone want incorporation to give Freddie and Perfecto Zizzbaum rights and obligations under the main agreement. What is going on here? Probably only drafting confusion.

Incorporation by reference can make sense if, for example, you want to place definitions that appear in multiple agreements in a single schedule that can then be incorporated into each agreement. But you don't *need* incorporation by reference. It's just as good—in fact, better—if each agreement provides that "except as otherwise stated, terms defined in schedule A are used in this agreement with the meanings given them in schedule A." Better because you have to think about what you're doing.

A final word for the calorie conscious: You can slim a document substantially by two-sided copying. One should have a care for the senior partner who must drag that documentary cinder block from office to home and back, his muscles aching, his spirits drained, with no solace other than the prospect of retribution at the morning floggings.[44]

---

43. 5 U.S.C. § 552(a).

44. Those wonderful names Frederick Threepwood and Perfecto Zizzbaum come from the works of P.G. Wodehouse.

BOILERPLATE

An agreement is the formalization of a business bargain, and every bargain is unique. Nonetheless, there are passages and provisions that seem to appear unchanged in almost all agreements. The usual legal nickname for these standard provisions is "boilerplate." Boilerplate provisions are seldom negotiated or even read carefully. It's simply assumed that they are embodiments of some high lawyer's art, a testimony to the wisdom of a succession of generations of master drafters.

In this chapter I'll take a long look at some current boilerplate. It turns out that much of it can be improved and some of it eliminated.

EXECUTION IN COUNTERPARTS

Tucked at the back of many agreements, you find these strange doings:

> This agreement may be executed in any number of counterparts and by different parties in separate counterparts. Each counterpart when so executed shall be deemed to be an original and all of which together shall constitute one and the same agreement.

What is going on here?

I haven't found much written on this "counterparts clause," but there seem to be two rationales. The first is that the counterpart clause "makes it clear that each party need not sign the same copy of the document in order to have a legally enforceable agreement."[45]

Suppose that Punch, Judy and you are the contracting parties. At the closing, each of you signs two copies of the agreement and gives one signed copy to each of the other two. Now Punch, Judy and you each have two copies, each signed by one of the other two parties. Will you need a counterparts clause to make the agreement enforceable?

There would be no problem if Punch, Judy and you had all signed the same copy of the document. But who says you didn't? Just remove the staples from your two copies, place the signature pages signed by Punch and Judy together with the other pages of one of the agreements *et voila!,* you have a copy signed by all the parties. Whether you have two copies, each signed by one party, or one copy signed by all the parties depends on how you wield your stapler. Is the counterparts clause really about *stapling!*?

Remember your contracts course? (I know it has been a long time and none of it ever proved the least bit useful before, but bear with me.) For a legally enforceable agreement, droned the professor, you need offer, acceptance, consideration, capacity and, if the agreement is subject to the statute of frauds, "a note or memorandum . . . subscribed by the party to be charged . . ." (this version from New York's General Obligations Law, § 5-701). I may have forgotten some other stuff, but I'm certain that enforceability never depended on staples.

In a large syndicated loan agreement there may be 60 parties with signatures spread over a dozen pages. Could anyone believe that the agreement might not be enforceable simply because everyone doesn't sign the same page? And if everyone doesn't have to sign the same page, why can't we have a separate signature page for each of the 60 parties (it's quite commonly done)? And if a separate signature page for each party is acceptable, why should it make a difference that each signature page also contains some other scribbling in the form of places for other parties to sign?

---

45. This is from a handbook on credit agreements put together by a large New York law firm.

I'm an in-house lawyer, and my time and facilities for legal research are limited, but such research as I've done has not disclosed any authority for the proposition that a counterparts clause is needed for an enforceable agreement. I did discover that over 100 years ago, the City Court of New York, Special Term, dismissed a complaint by a landlord who could only produce the counterpart of the lease signed by the tenant. But General Term reversed, citing a number of authorities to the effect that "where a contract is executed in counterparts, each party signing only the counterpart by which he is bound, and delivering such counterpart to the other party, each counterpart is primary evidence against the party signing it, and those claiming under him."[46] Obviously, there would have been no occasion to argue the evidence point if the contract was not legally enforceable.

This brings us to the law of evidence and the second rationale for the counterparts clause. The American Bar Foundation's Commentaries on the Model Debt Indenture Provisions states (p. 590) that:

> Typically, several copies of the Indenture will be fully executed and therefore it is highly desirable to include a provision relating to counterparts in order to avoid any problem as to which of the several signed copies of the Indenture is the original.

The Federal Rules of Evidence provide (§ 1002) that "to prove the content of a writing, the original writing is required." But an "original" of a writing is "the writing itself *or any counterpart* intended to have the same effect by a person executing it" (§ 1001, emphasis added).

Under the federal rules, counterparts are originals, so the counterparts clause is unnecessary. On this point, the federal rules are consistent with common law rules of evidence; it seems well settled that where there are multiple copies of an agreement, each executed by all the parties, each is an original agreement.

46. *Roosevelt v. Smith*, 40 N.Y.S. 381, 382 (1896).

Suppose you hold two copies of a contract with Punch and Judy, one of which has been manually signed by Punch and the other by Judy. You sue Punch for breach. If you didn't know any legal rules, would you take seriously Punch's argument that he is not bound by the contract that he signed because Judy signed a separate, although identical, piece of paper or that your document with Punch's signature isn't good evidence because Judy's signature is on a different piece of paper with identical terms? With common sense telling us that a counterparts clause plays no role, and the law in agreement, what is left for the counterparts clause?

One can imagine a time when the counterparts clause might have made sense. It's easy to forget, as laser printers and photocopiers spit out identical copies like popcorn, that an identical copy was once a rarity. To get one before 1900, you would have had to have the document typeset. (Carbon paper was available before 1850 but was messy and unsatisfactory until the early 1900s when Brazilian caranuba wax began to be added to the coating. Just thought you'd like to know.)

In the pre-carbon age, copying meant hand copying (with a pen or a typewriter), with the attendant danger of nonidentical copies. So if you wanted Punch and Judy each to have a copy of an agreement, but you didn't want to pay a printer or a gang of scriveners, you might have considered not repeating Punch's representations, warranties and covenants in his copy. Instead, Punch would take away a document signed by Judy that only showed Judy's representations, warranties and covenants, and Judy would have a document signed by Punch that showed only his representations, warranties and covenants.

Now each document is truly a counterpart of the other in the nonlegal sense of something that corresponds to, complements or completes the other—the sense in which an "identical counterpart" is a contradiction in terms. The only remaining problem is knowing what Punch's and Judy's counterparts are counterparts *of*.

Enter the indenture. In days of old the counterparts might be written at opposite ends of a single sheet of parchment and the two ends cut apart by a jagged or wavy line. The indentations made the document(s) an indenture. When the pieces were brought back together, the indentations would match them like the key to a lock. The same trick could be done with separate sheets of paper by simultaneously clipping their edge in an indented pattern.

If the indenture was a lease, the part signed by the grantor (the lessor or landlord) was called the original and the part signed by the tenant was called the counterpart. So one can understand how in 1896 a New York trial court faced with a counterpart signed by a tenant could hold that the document was not probative evidence. They got it wrong, but it was hardly a dishonorable mistake.

Having so little real work to occupy itself with, the modern counterparts clause tends to run with low company and get into trouble. In 1991, a corporate Punch and Judy each signed, at separate locations, a copy of a proposed agreement, and each left its copy with its lawyer. The signed copies were never exchanged. An Ohio appeals court, citing the documents' counterparts clause, held that the two undelivered copies formed one binding contract since the contract was not conditioned on delivery.[47] Now ain't law interesting?

WRINKLES IN THE ENFORCEABILITY BOILERPLATE

While munching through a typical credit agreement, you may come upon this paradoxical plum:

> Borrower warrants that this agreement is the legal, valid and binding obligation of borrower, enforceable in accordance with its terms.

What can it mean? If the agreement is unenforceable, won't the warranty be unenforceable as well? The sentence makes sense in a legal opinion, but placed in the agreement itself, it seems to

---

47. *Indus. Heat Treat. Co. v. Indus. Heat Treat.*, 104 Ohio App. 3d 499 (1995).

verge on self-contradiction. It's like the liar paradox: You can say that someone else always lies, but you can't say it about yourself.

There may be another way to read the warranty. There's been an east-coast/west-coast debate about what the sentence means in legal opinions, with easy-going Californians feeling that it's enough if the agreement is enforceable by-and-large, whereas buttoned-down New Yorkers insist that the sentence means that every last, little, itty-bitty provision of the agreement is enforceable. The New York interpretation may not be the most natural reading of the sentence, but it at least makes the sentence's appearance in an agreement logically inoffensive: In New York, at least, the borrower is warranting that every (other) provision in the agreement is enforceable.

Hold that thought while we look at two other typical provisions:

> If any provision in this agreement is held invalid, illegal or unenforceable in any respect, the legality, validity and enforceability of the remaining provisions in this agreement shall not in any way be affected or impaired thereby.

> If any warranty in this agreement is false in any material respect when made, the Lender may (i) terminate its commitment to lend and (ii) declare the outstanding loans immediately due and payable.

The first provision is usually referred to as a *severability* clause; the second is a radically simplified version of an *acceleration* clause.

It's beginning to make sense. If the entire agreement is unenforceable because, for example, it was not authorized or was signed by a six-year old, the enforceability warranty will also be unenforceable. If the lack of enforceability affects only a particular provision, however, then the severability clause will preserve the rest of the agreement. Among the survivors will be the enforceability warranty, which our borrower, Judy, will now have breached. That breach will enable Punch, the lender, to cut off Judy's line of credit and accelerate any outstanding loans under the surviving acceleration clause.

Wait a minute. The provisions that are likely to be unenforceable are those involving remedies—provisions for default interest, liquidated damages, foreclosure on collateral, and their ilk—and these were most likely drafted by Punch's lawyers. When it comes to remedies, lenders and their lawyers tend to take as much as they can—and then take more. Punch wants to get his toes as close to the line as possible, and he need not worry about stepping over because he can rely on the severability clause. So Punch will draft the documents aggressively.

Fine for Punch, and probably acceptable to Judy (most borrowers don't think a lot about life after default) except that it may allow Punch to pull the plug at any time based on some dodgy provision that Punch himself inserted into the agreement.

Could this really happen? Maybe not. I find it hard to believe that a court would allow Punch to cancel a line of credit and call a loan because he suddenly realizes that a provision *he drafted* is not enforceable. But I can't think of a good legal argument that gets me to that conclusion. Waiver arguments, for example, probably won't work because the agreement will no doubt have a provision that requires all waivers to be in writing. Nor am I confident that a court would find the quoted provisions to be unconscionable.

Will Punch's arguments fail because he has breached his duty of good faith and fair dealing?[48] Perhaps, but Punch can argue:

> Gee, your honor, I just took an old agreement off the shelf—it's really pretty much like everybody else's agreement—but when Judy started having problems, I read the agreement more carefully, and imagine my Surprise and Horror when I realized that one of the remedies was unenforceable! Of course, I had to call the loan.

I'm all choked up. But can any one say that Punch is being dishonest? Punch's story is all too plausible: The lawyers used several bits of venerable boilerplate without giving them a lot of thought. Only when matters escalated to DefCon3 did they sit

---

48. RESTATEMENT (SECOND) OF CONTRACTS § 205.

down and read the agreements *very* carefully. (These considerations also indicate that Punch would not be subject to an estoppel defense.)

Punch may, of course, have known from the outset that the provision might be unenforceable because Judy's counsel excepted it out of the legal opinion. Even if Punch hadn't a clue as to the possible unenforceability of a provision, however, you might argue that Punch should be charged with knowledge of what the document means. But then so should Judy. And this "charging with knowledge" business seems a little harsh when, in truth, almost no one knows what the document means. I only recently thought about the interrelations of the quoted provisions, and I may have misinterpreted them.

So how do you find out what the provisions mean? I don't know. There is little commentary on standard boilerplate and few cases. Lawyers may insist that a provision has "stood the test of time." This only means, however, that the provision has been around so long that no one in the room is old enough to know how it got there originally.

What can Judy do? Not much. Let's face it, there's a lot of law that's purely formalistic, and you are unlikely to get far arguing against it. The whole point of standard clauses is that, with so much more important stuff to deal with in the typical transaction, you don't want to waste time arguing about provisions that earlier generations of lawyers have fought and died for. Lives the lawyer who hath not said "Let's not reinventeth the wheel."

Unfortunately, the standard provisions may not be appropriate for every agreement. Consider the severability provision; sometimes you can't do without it. For example, in a security agreement, you'd much rather lose one of your remedies than find that your entire security interest has vanished. But even in a security agreement, you might regret having a severability clause if the unenforceable provision turned out to be the grant of the security interest itself.

The upshot is that sometimes you might prefer that the entire agreement become invalid rather than be stuck with an agreement without a clause that meant a lot to your side. It may therefore be better in many cases to leave out the severability clause and rely on the common law to sort out which provisions are an essential part of the agreed exchange. After all, the Restatement (Second) of Contracts provides at § 184 that:

> (1) If [for public policy reasons] less than all of an agreement is enforceable . . . , a court may nevertheless enforce the rest of the agreement in favor of a party who did not engage in serious misconduct if the performance as to which the agreement is unenforceable is not an essential part of the exchange.

> (2) A court may treat only part of a term as unenforceable under the rule stated in subsection (1) if the party who seeks to enforce the term obtained it in good faith and in accordance with reasonable standards of fair dealing.

The *Restatement* illustrates subsection (2) by a provision for an interest rate that exceeds the legal maximum. According to the *Restatement,* if the parties simply made an error in calculating the rate, the provision is enforceable up to the maximum legal rate. If the lender knew when the loan was made that the interest rate exceeded the legal maximum, however, the *Restatement's* view is that the entire provision for interest would be unenforceable.

So, unless you know exactly what you're doing—that is, you're dealing with a specific problem rather than just inserting the traditional boilerplate—it might be better to leave out the severability clause. (In fact, lots of lenders do without a severability clause, perhaps for this reason.) And don't posture by sticking in provisions you know are unenforceable.

DOES THE PONY EXPRESS STILL STOP HERE?

Here's a standard contract provision (from a big New York firm, tidied up somewhat):

> All notices shall be in writing (including telecopier, telegraphic or telex communication) and mailed, telecopied,

telegraphed, telexed or delivered to the relevant party at its address on schedule 1. Notices shall, when mailed, telecopied, telegraphed or telexed, be effective when deposited in the mails, telecopied, delivered to the telegraph company or confirmed by telex answerback, respectively.

Standard it may be, but does it make sense? In particular, why should a notice be effective when it's *sent* rather than when it's *received*?

Sometimes a notice has to be effective on sending. Section 222 of Delaware's General Corporation Law, for example, provides that notice of a stockholders' meeting must be given not less than 10 nor more than 60 days in advance and that the notice is given "when deposited in the United States mail, postage prepaid, directed to the stockholder at his address as it appears on the records of the corporation." With multiple stockholders, only the sending of the notice can provide a single reference point. Moreover, it may be unimportant if a few stockholders fail to receive the notice.

The contract provision quoted above is worded much like the Delaware stockholders' notice provision, but its application to a contract seems forced. The purpose of a notice is only achieved when the addressee reads it. Clearly, it is the sender of the notice who is best placed to make sure the notice arrives.

In negotiations, lawyers occasionally insist on this provision because they think their clients are more likely to be senders than recipients. The provision, they feel, will make a notice effective even if it never arrives; their clients can just fire and forget. Perhaps, but I would never place that much faith in the provision— is it a *notice* after all if it fails to notify?

Under section 1-201 of the Uniform Commercial Code, you notify someone if you take "such steps as may be reasonably required to inform the other in ordinary course whether or not such other actually comes to know of it." And section 1-101(3) states that notice delivered to an organization is "effective for a particular transaction from the time when it is brought to the attention of the individual conducting that transaction, and in any event from the time when it would have been brought to his attention if the organization had exercised due diligence . . ." These provisions can be varied by agreement, but they provide a baseline for the approach a court might take when Freddie claims he never got the notice.

I prefer to regard the effective-on-sending provision, like the Delaware stockholders' notice provision, as primarily concerned with timing: Assuming that the notice gets to its destination, it is the sending, not the receiving, that starts the clock ticking.

Somewhere behind the mists of time, a primordial lawyer hunkered down to chisel the first notice provision. Why did the lawyer choose to make notices effective on sending rather than receipt?

I suspect that our legal primitive began with an assumption about the method that would be used to send the notice and then worked back from the characteristics of the method to decide whether effectiveness on sending or receipt made more sense.

If that first notice provision was written any time before about 1960, our ur-lawyer (call him Urnie) probably assumed that notices would be *mailed*. Mail was cheap and left a written and signed record.

Urnie might have reasoned thusly: If a notice is sent by first class mail, it is difficult to fix the time of receipt. But there is an objective indicator of the time first-class mail is sent—the postmark. If I receive the notice, I know from the postmark when it was mailed and have the envelope as evidence; if I sent the notice, I know when it was mailed and can challenge the recipient to produce the postmarked envelope.

Urnie's reliance on the postmark may seem unrealistic, but he was probably making one more reasonable assumption: that anything mailed first-class would almost certainly be delivered the following day.

It is hard for us cynical moderns to realize the awe with which a more innocent time regarded the United States Post Office. My mother would recite with no trace of irony that "neither snow, nor rain nor something, something can stay these couriers from the swift completion of their appointed rounds."

Two random examples may illustrate the faith our elders had in their mail service: First, Berton Rouché in *The Medical Detectives* reports that in 1942 a doctor at New York's Metropolitan Hospital had to inform the Department of Health:

> ... to which the appearance of any disease of an epidemiological nature must be promptly communicated, that he had just uncovered a case of trichinosis. . . . The report of the arresting discovery at Metropolitan reached the Health Department on the morning of Friday, April 17 [the day after it was sent]. Its form was conventional—a postcard bearing a scribbled name, address and diagnosis.[49]

Second, I once read a profile of jeweler Harry Winston which revealed that Winston's standard method for shipping diamonds was to mail them. He claimed he never lost a stone.

Besides its touching faith in the reliability of the mails, the quoted notice provision bears other marks of its ancient provenance. I refer, of course, to the references to telex and telegraph. Today's preferred means for notices and other time sensitive communications are fax (which makes its way into the quoted notice provision by a reference, no doubt added recently, to "telecopier") and air courier (which may qualify under the provision as "mail"). I suppose we shall soon be giving notices by e-mail, a method not contemplated by the quoted notice provision.

Because the quoted provision specifies transmission *means* (mail, telecopy, telex, etc.) rather than transmission *results* (confrontation with addressee eyeball), it does not adapt well to new technologies. A more flexible notice provision might be achieved by requiring the notice to be a "record" as defined in section 9-102 of the Uniform Commercial Code:

> "Record" . . . means information that is inscribed on a tangible medium or which is stored in an electronic or other medium and is retrievable in perceivable form.

49. BERTON ROUECHÉ, THE MEDICAL DETECTIVES 16–19 (1980).

I didn't ride all this way, however, just to present a better notice provision. In any scheme of things, notice provisions aren't that important. What I hope to deliver is an object lesson.

Urnie the atturney's notice provision was, for its time and place, a solid piece of drafting. But Urnie retired to the sun belt many years ago. The technologies that are familiar to us were unknown in Urnie's heyday, and we now have much less faith in the institution—the US Post Office (now the US Postal Service)—on which he relied.

Like Urnie, we shall always draft provisions based on the world we know. We can draft flexibly, and we can provide some leeway for technical and social change, but we are likely to be wrong in much of our thinking about the future.

Legal boilerplate is neither mumbo-jumbo nor holy writ. It represents, for the most part, a drafter's reasonable attempt to deal with features of a legal, business, social and technological environment. As that environment changes, well-drafted provisions can become unsuitable. Unfortunately, the ancient provisions don't come with commentary. An associate plodding through the firm's form file is unlikely to know what assumptions underlay the provisions. Perhaps an obscure phrase is there to deal with a legal problem that remains formidable. This possibility renders many lawyers reluctant to tamper with the hallowed hokum. But the obscure provision may just as likely have been written to deal with bustles or buggy whips.

The conclusion is depressing: Safety does *not* lie in reciting the standard phrases. Perhaps the provisions were drafted by geniuses, but those geniuses may have been wearing powdered wigs.

It would be nice if there was a committee (I am *not* volunteering) that published revised boilerplate provisions on an ongoing basis, with commentary to explain why certain choices were made. Until then, the only solution is to think clearly and act bravely. *Courage, mes petits!*

EXPLAINING WITH EXAMPLES

Agreements seldom contain any explanatory material such as commentary, examples or other bits of the standard paraphernalia of explanation and clarification. Why not?

Contrast agreements with statutes. Does anyone think that the UCC would be clearer if we deleted the official comments? If comments make the UCC clearer, why don't lawyers use commentary in their agreements?

I think the lawyer's answer would be that businesspeople phrase their agreement in terms of principles and outcomes. The drafter's task, however, is to clarify the business bargain by thinking through the particular actions that will be required to achieve the businesspeople's goals. Precise drafting requires setting down instructions to individuals or organizations to perform particular actions in specified circumstances.

An obvious analogy to the legal drafter is the computer programmer. A programming project begins with a description of goals to be achieved and it ends with the actual program— detailed and precise instructions (in a programming language) to be performed by a computer. In between falls the discipline of programming. In writing the program, the programmer is forced to confront and resolve all the latent ambiguities and conflicts in the initial statement of objectives.

DRAFTING-AS-PROGRAMMING

The legal drafter is the programmer of the business bargain. As the drafter thinks through the problems involved in reducing an informal agreement on principles and outcomes to a set of instructions, she identifies problems that escaped the notice of the parties. In the discipline of drafting-as-programming, the lawyer both memorializes and makes workable the intention of the parties.

Basking in this sunny view of the lawyer's role, we may come to believe that statements of objectives, examples and commentary have no place in the agreement. It is easy to conclude that, just as the computer's operations can only be governed by its precisely written program, so the business bargain should only be governed by the drafter's program-like instructions.

Such a view fails to realize all the implications of the programming analogy. In legal drafting, as in computer programming, the price of clarity is fragility. Precisely worded instructions in computer programs and in agreements often fail to work as intended.

When a program freezes, someone has to figure out what the program meant to do in the large and also what the intention was behind the bits and pieces. The operative language (the program) may be the object of the exercise, but it doesn't tell the whole story. The statement of overall objectives, the flowcharts and the programmer's remarks are all descriptions at various levels of specificity, each having its own uses and importance. When things go wrong, the programmer must reconsider the flowcharts and other statements of goals and objectives.

You never know if a program has frozen unless you know what it was intended to do. Perhaps the apparently anomalous result was the real objective. (As they say at Microsoft, "It's not a bug, it's a feature!") Similarly, you don't know if an agreement is drafted correctly unless you know what was intended by the parties. But lawyers, unlike programmers, deliberately cut themselves off from all help outside the document. If you take seriously admonitions that "this document contains the entire agreement of the parties," then you will want the agreement to contain both the tightly drafted "program" and some less precise statements of the business bargain. The "programming language" bits of the agreement clarify the statement of the business bargain, but it works the other way as well.

Explanation isn't all one way. We explain things at many levels of generality and precision, and every level adds something. If you have to explain an agreement with examples and commentary (and you usually do), it's time to consider whether the best place for the examples and commentary might not be the agreement itself.

A simple example: Two affiliated borrowers under a revolving credit agreement, Titan Corp. and Midget Enterprises, separately agree that Titan will borrow no more than 60% of the amount available under the facility and Midget will draw no more than 40%. The credit agreement, however, requires Titan to pay all facility and administrative fees, so a side agreement between the borrowers provides that Midget will reimburse Titan for Midget's share of the fees. You could draft the side agreement to say:

> Whenever Titan pays a facility or administrative fee, Midget will reimburse Titan for 40% of the payment.

but it is probably better to draft it like this:

> The borrowers intend that all administrative and facility fees be borne by them in proportion to the maximum amount each is permitted to borrow under the revolving credit agreement. Accordingly, whenever Titan pays a facility or administrative fee, . . . [etc.].

THE CAST OF CHARACTERS

There is an art to constructing examples; this section will essay some tricks for naming the *dramatis personae.*

An example in the prefatory note to article 4A, "funds transfers," of the Uniform Commercial Code begins in the following folksy way:

> X, a debtor, wants to pay an obligation owed to Y . . . .

Stop right there. Do you know anyone named X? How many people do you know who even have an initial X (and whose first name isn't Francis)?

The problem with X and Y isn't just that they're bloodless (what kind of person do you imagine X to be? How different is he or she from Y?), but that they're easily confused. Midway through the paragraph (which, on a quick count, contained 42 Xs and Ys), you may forget who is the debtor and who the creditor.

Compare the above example with one from the official comment to section 9-328 of the UCC:

> . . . Debtor owns 1,000 shares of XYZ stock held through a securities account with Able & Co. . . . Debtor borrows from Beta [Bank] and grants Beta a security interest in 1,000 shares of XYZ Co. stock. . . .

Notice the superiority of the "Debtor-meets-Able & Co." nomenclature. Debtor identifies the role of the character and is, in addition, an unlikely name for a brokerage firm. Able & Co., in contrast, could plausibly be the name of a brokerage firm but not of a bank, a widget manufacturer or a law firm.

Not all the names in the example above are so felicitous. The official comment to the section uses Beta and, elsewhere, Alpha, as bank names. Nothing in those words suggests banks. Better names would be "First National" and "Second National." Furthermore, if it's important to distinguish one bank from the other, city names may help—Yuma National Bank has a different feel from Penobscot National.

Similarly, XYZ Co. is not the best name for the company whose shares are to be pledged. XYZ Motors would be better, and Standard Motors would be better yet. The word "Motors" suggests an entity that is unlikely to be a customer, a brokerage firm or a bank.

Unlikely, but not impossible. Motor car companies and banks can be customers of brokerage firms, and a brokerage firm might have a name like Standard or First National (although Debtor remains implausible). But Able & Co. for the brokerage, First National for the Bank and Standard Motors for the securities issuer are names that fit smoothly into familiar story lines.

By "story lines" I mean the internalized pictures of the world involved in so much of our thinking. Story lines aren't usually fictitious, although they usually aren't exactly true. As our mental powers grow through education and experience, our story lines take on greater complexity and adaptability. We leave the good-guy, bad-guy simplicities of childhood for a more mature and nuanced picture of life's complexities. But we may still be familiar with some simple story lines that we don't necessarily believe.

For example, there's a familiar story line—call it a *stereotype*—that accountants are dull, dry, meticulous "bean-counters." This stereotype doesn't conform to my experience, and possibly not to yours, but the stereotype does not have to be believed to be useful. In developing my example, my accountant is more likely to have a name like Elmer Precision than Lance Almost. As I work through the example, it's unlikely that anyone will forget that Elmer is the accountant (although if the example involved accounting error or hanky-panky, a name like Jerry Jugglemeister might be better).

Looking back at our "Debtor meets Able & Co." example, we may wonder whether the name Debtor is the best solution. A better solution might be to call our debtor Mr. Micawber or Spendthrift or some other name that reliably suggests straitened circumstances.

Using a storyline or stereotype helps the reader follow a complicated example. But there is a controversial issue in using stereotypes that must be faced. In the prevailing story line, accountants are not only dull and dry, they are also male and white.

About race and ethnicity, I shall say little. Unless you work at it, first names give few clues to race or ethnicity. The same is true for invented surnames like Precision and Almost. And in America at least, an "American" last name like Able stands more for a bland uniformity than for a particular ethnic group, such as Anglo-Saxons.

In contrast, gender issues in naming are unavoidable. You could, of course, call your characters Precision and Almost *tout court,* but that is hardly an improvement over calling them X and Y. Story lines need people, not placeholders.

So, in constructing your example, should your accountant be Elmer Precision or Pricilla Sharp-Pencil?

It all depends. If you're trying to guide your reader through some ultra-tricky terrain, go with Elmer. Your reader may already have enough to absorb without the distraction of having his consciousness raised.

If, on the other hand, the terrain is not that difficult, you should seriously consider some stereotype demolition. But don't just call your accountant Pricilla Sharp-Pencil. If you're going to bash the accountancy stereotype altogether, go the whole hog: This is a job for Sheena Starr, CPA.

The point that I'm making is about writing, not political correctness. Writing requires decisions about when your readers should be carried along by the current of a stereotype and when they should be forced to swim against it. And there's often much to be gained by heading upstream.

The Front Page by Ben Hecht and Charles MacArthur is a frequently revived 1920s play about Chicago newspapermen. Its hero is Hildy (Harold?) Johnson, a quick-witted and none-too-scrupulous master of the arts of yellow journalism. Part of the play involves his ambivalent feelings about his fiancée, who wants him to marry, settle down and live a regular life.

When Howard Hawks and Charles Lederer brought *The Front Page* to the screen (for the second time), they stumbled upon the idea of having Hildy played by Rosalind Russell, with Ralph Bellamy as the fiancée. The film was released in 1940 as *His Girl Friday.*

I have nothing perceptive to say about the mechanisms at work in our reacting to reversals of gender stereotypes, but it's hard to ignore the effects: *His Girl Friday* has a snap and sparkle that more faithful renditions of *The Front Page* lack. (The effect of the gender swap may have been even more powerful in the 1940s when there were fewer female professionals.)

The lesson is that if you have a feel for stereotypes, you can use them to reduce the reader's burden of understanding or increase the reader's enjoyment and awareness by cutting against them.

In peopling your examples, you should watch out that your protagonists don't have names that are distracting. In discussing guaranties (in "Other Documents," below), I use Worrywart as the company that receives the guaranty. When I was writing that section, however, I initially called the company Shylock Corp. Shylock is, of course, the most famous receiver of a guaranty in literature. But Shylock is also the villain in a play widely regarded as anti-Semitic. Being Jewish myself, I wasn't too worried about charges of anti-Semitism (and I love *The Merchant of Venice* despite all), but I eventually decided that using Shylock would simply be too distracting for many readers.

A more humdrum example of the same phenomenon is found in the preceding section. I used an example with a "Titan Corp." The example originally appeared in an article with the company named "Titanic Corp." Since the article appeared, the movie *Titanic* has induced a wave of interest in the great ship. Although Titanic Corp. was acceptable when written, today it would suggest disaster at sea, young lovers parted, box-office receipts—all topics unrelated to my purpose, so I changed it.

One final practical tip on naming protagonists is that, if there are two individuals, make one a man and one a woman. This may give you the opportunity to exploit the old boy-meets-girl story line, but there's a more prosaic consideration: Two differently sexed characters allows you to use gender-specific pronouns—he, she, his, her, etc.—without ambiguity.

FUN (AND GRIEF) WITH ALGEBRA

The pooling and servicing agreement for a credit card securitization provides for monthly interest payments to the class A certificates equal to:

> the product of (i) the product of (x) the class A certificate rate and (y) a fraction the numerator of which is the actual number of days in the related interest period and the denominator of which is 360 and (ii) the class A principal balance as of the close of business on the last day of the preceding monthly period. . . .

You've probably seen thousands of similar provisions. If you're feeling conscientious, you stop, pick up your pencil and, on a legal pad, you reverse engineer the provision into something like:

$$\frac{\text{class A}}{\text{certificate rate}} \times \frac{\text{number of days in interest period}}{360} \times \frac{\text{class A}}{\text{principal balance}}$$

We learned the arithmetical notation for equations in elementary school. Unlike the lawyer's word version, arithmetical notation is almost instantly comprehensible. It would be impossible to do any complex mathematics if we were limited to the word versions that stalk legal agreements. Indeed, the use of verbal formulations rather than arithmetical notation is a prime contributor to the opacity of many agreements. So why didn't the drafter use arithmetical notation?

One answer I have heard is that lawyers are, as a group, a tad weak in arithmetic. Words are our delight, but numbers supposedly frighten us.

I'm suspicious of such a generalization, but we need not decide the issue here because I'm not talking about lawyers generally. If a lawyer is not comfortable with arithmetical relations, he's going to put all the distance possible between himself and the nearest pooling and servicing agreement. He certainly will not be found drafting such a document.

A more convincing explanation is that lawyers draft that way because that's the way they're taught. We learn to draft by reading the documents that went before us, and lawyers have been describing numerical relationships in tortured prose for decades.

But that just postpones the question. There must have been a distant time when Urnie, our ur-lawyer, first had to include an equation in a document. I've got to believe that Urnie first structured the quoted provision, or its paleolithic predecessor, in arithmetical notation. Why did he then recast it in lawyer-speak?

Perhaps Urnie tried to use arithmetical notation but failed because his secretary, Ureka, couldn't adequately produce it with the technology of her time, the typewriter. With planning and patience, Ureka might have produced something like:

Monthly interest = class A certificate rate
$$X \text{ (number of days in interest period } /360)$$
$$X \text{ class A principal balance}$$

Not bad, but not as instantly comprehensible as our first version. The difference is that, unlike Ureka, I had available all the resources of a modern word processing program, including an equation editor.

These days, Ureka is a lawyer, not a secretary, but she still does the typing (although we now call it word processing), and she still bangs out the equations in words. Like most lawyers, she is probably modifying an existing document. Ureka doesn't know why the document she starts with describes arithmetical relations in words rather than arithmetical notations. If she's like most lawyers—and most lawyers are—she doesn't ponder long on the technological constraints of bygone legal practice. She probably just assumes that the convoluted prose descriptions of numerical relationships represent legal, not technological, requirements.

In any case, prudence dictates that Ureka not attempt to recast the entire document but simply change a few words here and there. After all, her clients are unlikely to indulge her by paying the fees and enduring the delays that a full-scale rewrite would entail. Recasting a document only makes sense at an enterprise level where the costs can be spread out over many documents and clients.

It would be nice to think that lawyers hang on to outmoded conventions simply out of solicitude for their clients. But there is a larger cause for Ureka's caution: Fear. The idea that a court would reject a contractual provision because it uses arithmetical notation familiar from grammar school, rather than word formulations only found in legal agreements, is nonsense. (Not so nonsensical, of course, that some judge somewhere might take such a position. When you're dealing with the wackier fringes of the judiciary, however, all bets are off; arithmetical notation is just as likely to help as hurt you.)

Nonetheless, Ureka's fear that a court might take such a position is part of legal culture, and that culture begins in law school.

One of the first things Ureka learned in law school was caution. Legal eaglets are regaled with stories of lawyers who totaled the client's Ferrari because they missed some legal nicety. "Be careful out there!" is the constant message. No stories are told of lawyers who were right to take a chance—that is, to balance legal concerns against practical business concerns and to find the legal concerns wanting. The law school ethos, if it were applied to physicians, would be: Don't operate, don't medicate!

Caution can lead to paralysis: In the crucible of battle ("Have that draft agreement on my desk at oh-nine-hundred!"), the raw recruits freeze up. Knowing she has to do something, yet afraid to do anything, Ureka, the associate, makes the minimal changes possible. Heinrich, the surgical intern, faces larger terrors, and probably responds no better. But Heinrich's culture is overtly interventionist, so his errors are likely to be of commission rather than omission. With luck, Ureka's errors will not be noticed, and Heinrich's will be buried.

One day, Ureka is a partner, but the culture of caution remains. For one thing, she has behind her a body of cautious work in which she is likely to take some pride. Moreover, she now has a new source of anxiety—malpractice suits. What if something should go wrong with the new-fangled document? Better to rely on the tried, true and as yet unsued-upon standbys.

But, hey, you and me, we're better than that. We want to lead the world to a better tomorrow. We want to shake off the fetters of convention, seize the opportunities, to be . . . heroes! And we'd prefer to do it without taking any chances. What safer way than using arithmetical notation?

There is of, course, a downside to using arithmetical notation. For one thing, equation editors can be extremely clunky. More important, arithmetical notation can be drafted as poorly as any other provision. Consider the following example from a recent prospectus for medium term notes. Some of those notes are issued at a "commercial paper rate," plus or minus a spread. The prospectus defines the commercial paper rate for a note as the *money market yield* for that note, which it in turn defines as (stand back, folks):

$$\frac{D \times 360}{360 - (D \times M)} \times 100$$

> where "D" is the per annum rate for commercial paper quoted on a bank discount basis (expressed as a decimal), and "M" is the number of days in the period for which interest is being calculated.

Well, that's unenlightening. The formula isn't very complicated, and the term "money market yield" and the formula come straight out of a standard text, but that doesn't make it any easier to understand. Consider the numerator of the fraction. Even if you know what a rate quoted on a "bank discount basis" is, what do you get when you multiply it by 360? A number, no doubt, but not a meaningful one. It's not a price, or a discount or anything else with a natural meaning. It's just a number that inexplicably appears in a formula.

The denominator, 360 − (D × M), isn't any clearer. As we'll see, 360 is the number of days in the short year adopted for many money market instruments. But why are we deducting D x M from that number? The result is not going to be a number of days or anything else that is familiar.

This kind of thing could give algebra a bad name. Let's try to straighten this out, beginning with a little introduction to money market terminology.

Suppose Irma Investor buys a Prestodigimatics, Inc. note for $1,000. A year hence, Presto pays Irma $1,000 along with $60 interest. Then Irma's investment has an annual yield of:

$$\frac{\$60}{\$1,000}$$

which is 0.06. To change the decimal yield to a percentage, we multiply by 100:

$$\frac{\$60}{\$1,000} \times 100$$

which gives 6%.

The example is simple, not least because I assumed that Irma received her $60 in interest after exactly one year. Suppose, however, that Irma received her $60 in interest after only 300 days. What is the annual yield on her investment?

To calculate Irma's *annual* yield, we first calculate her *daily* yield by dividing the 6% yield by 300 days—the term of her investment—and then multiplying by 365—the number of days in the year. The formula looks like this:

$$\frac{\$60}{\$1,000} \times 100 \times \frac{365 \text{ days}}{300 \text{ days}}$$

which gives an annual yield of 7.3%.

Generalizing, we can say that the annual yield is:

$$\frac{\$ \text{ interest received}}{\$ \text{ investment}} \times \frac{\text{days in year}}{\text{term of instrument}} \times 100$$

As is well known, our unruly planet makes its annual circuit of the Sun in a bit more than 365 days, with the result that every fourth year has to have 366 days rather than 365. To smooth out this awkwardness, and to simplify some other calculations, the yield on many instruments is calculated on a year of 360 days. (Today, when our children are born with silver HP-12s clutched in their little fists, it may be difficult to appreciate that there was a time when the calculations were done by hand, usually with the aid of elaborate tables. In our computerized age, the 360-day year remains, perhaps because it gives lenders a bit of extra interest—sort of like the quaint British pre-decimal practice of quoting prices in guineas rather than pounds.)

If we calculate yield based on a year of 360 days, our annual yield formula becomes:

$$\frac{\$\text{ interest received}}{\$\text{ investment}} \times \frac{360}{\text{term of instrument}} \times 100$$

Annual yield on an investment over a year of 360 days is referred to in the markets as *money market yield.*

Commercial paper and certain other short-term instruments (most notably, Treasury bills) do not pay interest in the conventional sense. If Irma buys a $1,000 face amount commercial paper note, she will only receive the face amount—$1,000—at maturity. No interest. For Irma to make a profit, she must pay less than $1,000 for the note. Suppose Irma pays $980 for a $1,000 note that will mature in 90 days. Then the $20 difference between the price Irma pays and the $1,000 face amount of the note that she will receive at maturity is the *discount*. These types of instruments are usually referred to as *discount paper.*

Our money-market yield formula also works for discount paper. We just have to realize that the discount—in our example, the $20 difference between the price Irma pays and the amount she receives at maturity—is the interest, whereas the $980 Irma pays is the investment. Plugging the numbers into our formula gives:

$$\frac{\$20}{\$980} \times \frac{360}{90} \times 100$$

which (trust me) works out to a money market yield on Irma's commercial paper note of about 8.163%.

We'd be finished now, except that commercial paper prices are seldom quoted in terms of *dollar* discounts. Instead, they are quoted in terms of annual discount *rates*. For example, Irma's $20 discount on a $1,000 face amount commercial paper note is obviously a 2% discount rate (nonannualized). To get the annual discount rate, we divide by 90 (to get the daily discount rate), and then multiply by 360. This gives:

$$2\% \times \frac{360}{90}$$

or 8%. The annual discount rate for a 360-day year is the *bank discount rate*. (The bank discount rate is always lower than the money market yield because the former divides the discount by the face amount, whereas the latter divides by the face amount *less the discount*.)

Our problem now is how to convert the bank discount rate (in our example, 8%) into the money market yield (in our example, 8.163%).

No problem. Because we computed the bank discount rate from the dollar discount and the investment, all we have to do is reverse the process. In particular,

$$\$\text{ discount} = \frac{\$\text{ face}}{\text{amount}} \times \frac{\text{bank}}{\text{discount}} \times \frac{\text{term of instrument}}{360}$$
$$\text{rate}$$

All that is left now to derive the formula in the prospectus are a few algebraic manipulations. The details are a bit messy and not very interesting, so I've demoted them to an appendix. (I won't be devastated if you skip it.)

My point, however, is that things are clearer if you *don't* do the manipulations. The only reason for the appendix is to convince you (and myself) that our earlier money market yield formula works. For prospectus purposes, we might be better advised to simply say that:

Annual yield (over a year of 360 days) for a commercial paper instrument ("money market yield") may be computed by the formula:

$$\frac{\$ \text{ discount}}{\begin{array}{l}\$ \text{ face amount} \\ \text{of instrument}\end{array} - \$ \text{ discount}} \times \frac{360}{\begin{array}{c}\text{remaining term} \\ \text{of instrument}\end{array}} \times 100$$

where the $ discount is computed by the formula:

$$\begin{array}{l}\$ \text{ face amount} \\ \text{of instrument}\end{array} \times \begin{array}{l}\text{bank} \\ \text{discount} \\ \text{rate}\end{array} \times \frac{\text{remaining term of instrument}}{360}$$

and the bank discount rate is the percentage discount on the instrument, annualized over a year of 360 days.

This isn't a formula found in finance texts, and it takes longer to punch into a calculator, but it is easier to understand. For one thing, it explains "bank discount rate." More importantly, it doesn't group items in ways that are inscrutable; numerators and denominators correspond to well understood concepts.

APPENDIX: THE MESSY DETAILS

The money market yield formula is:

$$\frac{\$ \text{ interest received}}{\$ \text{ investment}} \times \frac{360}{\text{term of instrument}} \times 100$$

and the dollar discount formula is:

$$\$ \text{ discount} = \begin{array}{l}\$ \text{ face} \\ \text{amount}\end{array} \times \begin{array}{l}\text{bank} \\ \text{discount rate}\end{array} \times \frac{\text{term of instrument}}{360}$$

Because we're interested in the money market yield, which is a *rate* and not a dollar *amount,* we can compute the dollar discount on a standard face amount of $1. There are obvious simplifications in multiplying or dividing by one. Substituting our $ discount formula for "$ interest received" in our market yield formula, with a $1 face amount, and replacing "$ investment" with the face amount ($1) minus the formula for dollar discount, gives:

$$\frac{\$1 \times \frac{\text{bank}}{\text{discount rate}} \times \frac{\text{term of instrument}}{360}}{\$1 - \left(\$1 \times \frac{\text{bank}}{\text{discount rate}} \times \frac{\text{term of instrument}}{360}\right)} \times \frac{360}{\text{term of instrument}} \times 100$$

Canceling the "$" signs and the extraneous multiplications by one and substituting "D" for "bank discount rate" and "M" (think "**M**aturity") for the term of the instrument gives:

$$\frac{D \times \frac{M}{360}}{1 - \left(D \times \frac{M}{360}\right)} \times \frac{360}{M} \times 100$$

Multiplying the two fractions gives:

$$\frac{D \times \frac{M}{360} \times 360}{\left(1 - \left(D \times \frac{M}{360}\right)\right) \times M} \times 100$$

Canceling the "360"s and the "M"s gives:

$$\frac{D}{1 - \left(D \times \frac{M}{360}\right)} \times 100$$

Now multiply the numerator and denominator by 360 to get:

$$\frac{D \times 360}{360 - (D \times M)} \times 100$$

which is the text book and prospectus formula.

THE SECURITIES PROSPECTUS

Since 1993, I've written three to four short articles a year on legal writing. Throughout those years, I've worried from time to time that one day I would run out of material.

Although examples of bad writing cascade onto my desk every day, I feared—still fear—that the new bad writing would have much the same causes and cures as the old bad writing. I thought that when the current material petered out, however, I could turn to a rich new vein: I could write about securities prospectuses.

I was not a securities lawyer, so I was hesitant to write about an area in which I had little experience. If I were truly desperate, however, I thought I could always go prospecting in the nearest prospectus. After all, like you I have tried to read prospectuses and other disclosure documents and been amazed at the barriers to comprehension. In 1996 I wrote a column at my editor's request on securities prospectuses for a *Business Law Today* issue on securities law; however, I felt that I had merely knocked off a few nuggets from the mother lode.[50]

Then it all changed. First, the Securities and Exchange Commission adopted a "plain English" rule.[51] They even produced their own handbook on how to write plain English.[52] It didn't take away my livelihood, but it certainly threatened to take away my emergency stash. In theory, I could still write about bad

---

50. Howard Darmstadter, *A Prospectus for the Rest of Us,* BUS. L. TODAY, Jan.–Feb. 1996, at 40-41.

51. Rule 421(b) and (d) under the Securities Act of 1933.

52. HANDBOOK, *supra* note 28, at 22.

prospectus writing, but now I would be merely reinforcing principles propounded by securities regulators. Where's the fun in that? It seemed an activity in which I could learn or teach little.

Second, I became a securities lawyer, sort of. As part of an internal reorganization of my department, I was asked to work with the securitization folks. My first job was to turn our traditional prospectuses for securities backed by credit card receivables and residential mortgages into "plain English" prospectuses. What follows are my observations on prospectus writing in the plain English era. I begin with a description of how things were in the days before the plain English rule.

THE GOOD OL' DAYS

For that 1996 issue of *Business Law Today,* I was asked to give my views on the readability of the standard securities prospectus. It was hog heaven. Soooooo-wheeeee!

After the high came the hangover. Prospectuses certainly seemed an easy target, but how could I beat up on them unless I knew who read them and why? If the only people who read prospectuses were financial analysts and class-action lawyers, it might not have mattered that the documents were unreadable.

So, who reads prospectuses? And who might read them if the prose were clear and lively and the format more inviting? No one seemed to know, at least no one who actually wrote prospectuses. Admittedly, I only asked a handful of people, but I assume that information of this sort, if it were available, would get around quickly. No one I talked to could remember reading any empirical studies of prospectus usage. In addition, no one buys a prospectus. There are no letters-to-the-editor columns where prospectus readers can object to some disclosure inadequacy. No hard-driving publishers (or underwriters) seek to revamp the format to entice more business. The SEC was not encouraging companies to experiment with different sorts of prospectuses. In short, our knowledge of the actual or potential prospectus audience was anecdotal.

Faced with this lack of data, I had little choice but to accept the prevailing orthodoxy that prospectuses were to be read by a wide range of potential investors, from institutional investors to retired postal workers. How well did prospectuses answer to the varying needs and sophistication of all those potential readers?

In theory, it shouldn't have been too difficult. Newspapers are read by a wide range of people who even pay for the experience. Accordingly, newspapers are laid out to accommodate all these readers. If you don't read the financial pages, they can be easily avoided. If you're looking for the score of last night's game, it can be found in seconds.

Several factors help newspapers serve differing readers. First, people tend to read the same newspaper every day, so its organization becomes familiar—sports in section C, stock prices in section D and so forth. Even unfamiliar newspapers tend to be organized similarly; the most important news will be on the front page, with the most important story (for most readers) in the right hand column under the most eye-catching headline. Newspapers also use graphics to identify subject matter and convey information. The three-column photo of the close play at home tells you that this is the sports page; the graphs of stock prices tell you it's the financial page and provide valuable information to those who are interested.

Prospectuses are organized similarly. I looked at (but couldn't read) two initial public offering prospectuses from different underwriters and law firms, and the organizational similarities were striking. Those familiar with IPO prospectuses should have had little trouble finding the materials that interested them most.

Everybody else had to struggle, however. The SEC had decided that for those who were not connoisseurs of prospectuses, the most important sections were the "risk factors" section and the summary. Of course, no one knew then, or knows now, what people actually read. One can imagine ranges of people who are not familiar with prospectuses but who want to read material other than risk factors or a summary. For example, employees of the issuer or companies in the same line of business may want to base their investment decisions on an analysis of the issuer's technology and marketing plans. These readers may be sophisticated readers of parts of the prospectuses yet find other parts incomprehensible.

The old-style prospectus did a poor job of orienting readers unfamiliar with standard prospectus topography. For one thing, the table of contents was in an unlikely place—the back cover. So my first suggestion for improving the prospectus was to move the table of contents to the front cover. A new reader would be unlikely to miss it there.

Of course, as many others had noted, the prospectus front cover was already crowded with other guff, most of which could have been moved or dispensed with altogether. The front cover is the first thing the reader sees and should contain the most essential information with minimum distractions. Of the items that adorned the front page, I suggested keeping only the company name and logo, the title of the securities being offered, the date, the price and company proceeds (but without the footnotes) and the lead underwriters' names. I also suggested adding a table of contents and the company's address and phone number. (I'm guessing along with everyone else, but I think readers want to know where a company is located and the phone number of its investor relations department. This information was usually consigned to the tail end of the summary.)

After the front cover came the inside front cover. Here the news was good. The prospectuses I saw had photos of the company products on the inside front and back covers. One in particular impressed me: The company's primary product resting on what was recognizably a human fingertip. You can learn a lot from pictures. (There was also a full caps "stabilization" disclosure, which I believe was read only by people who didn't understand it.)

This brings us to the summary. Most people think of the summary as a sort of mini-prospectus for the least-sophisticated investors. But what was an unsophisticated (or semi-sophisticated) investor to make of the sentence that began "The Company employs dielectric isolation complementary bipolar technology . . ."? Was this technology *dernier cri* at MIT or *infra dig* in Novgorod?

To my way of thinking, the summary should be a guide to the rest of the prospectus. The table of contents ought to be skeletal; the summary should be used to give the next level of detail. Summary headings would correspond to the sections of the prospectus, with sketches of the most important information and cross-references (with page numbers!) to the more detailed descriptions.

Incidentally, every prospectus is accompanied by a summary that gives the most essential information in digestible form. These summaries are well organized, some with excellent tabular and graphical presentations of information. *But investors aren't allowed to see them!* I'm talking of the confidential memoranda managing underwriters give to their brokers to educate them about the offering. The memoranda are marked "for internal use only" in huge block letters and state that "this information may not be copied, distributed or shown to clients." Liability fears ensure that these useful documents are never seen by the public.

Enough of this balanced approach, I'm giving in to temptation. Most prospectuses read like "spot the dumb idea" puzzles. On the front page, I noted the following lawyer's tics: A heading "3,600,000 Shares Prestodigimatics Common Stock" is followed by "(par value $0.001 per share)." Who cares? And why was the date of the prospectus preceded by the hypo-informative "The date of this prospectus is . . ."?

More substantively, the headings in the summary of one prospectus formed the first words of the section, their function indicated only by italics. Tasteful, but nearly invisible. Another prospectus was entirely in sans serif type, giving joy no doubt to the optometric community. And both prospectuses, like every prospectus I had ever seen, were laid out in 6½ inch lines of 10-point type. No one should be asked to read lines that long. Why didn't prospectuses use columns like every magazine that is printed on similarly sized paper?

What did "Prestodigimatics™ is a trademark of the Company" add to "Prestodigimatics™"? Would anyone think it was Coca-Cola's trademark? And if you didn't know what "™" meant, were you likely to know what "trademark" meant?

How about "The following summary is qualified in its entirety by the more detailed information and consolidated financial statement including the notes thereto appearing elsewhere in this prospectus." Didn't anyone tell the writer what "summary" means? Could someone believe that a security was risky if reading the "risk factors" section put him to sleep?

That felt good. As I've said, there was lots more gold in them thar hills. Unfortunately, mining it would have involved reading more prospectuses, and I was not about to put myself through any more of that. So I left my readers with a wacky two-step idea for prospectus reform: First, get rid of all liability for prospectus contents except the issuer's liability for out-and-out fraud. This might free-up prospectus writing. Second, permit underwriters to disclose the performance of their offerings under some standardized measure. This might make the underwriter's name a seal of quality, thus rewarding underwriters for their talents in evaluating potential offerings.

And then along came the plain-English rule.

Toward a Plain English Prospectus

The SEC is now trying to make prospectuses, merger proxies and the like more accessible to stockholders, and I gather there is a determination at the Commission to clean up it's own act. We are promised that the Commission's own rules and releases will be done in a more reader-friendly style. Perhaps the Commission's review practices will also smile on certain forms of innovation.

What's missing is any admission that there may be deeper reasons for the turgidity of prospectus writing. One reason may be habit, and the plain-English rule has probably had some good effects there. But I suspect that the current litigation environment has played a major role in forming the securities prospectus. If so, it's a problem that can only partially be cured by the rule, although I applaud the SEC for trying.

Let's shove these doubts aside and get down to Howard's Handy Hints. Writing an investor-friendly prospectus involves breaking some old-style lawyerly habits. When Maybelle Buffet opens a prospectus or merger proxy, she does so as an investor, not a lawyer. Good legal writing may be confusing and irrelevant to her.

The deal isn't the documents. As a lawyer, you understand the transaction as a web of legal rights and obligations that are embodied in legal documents such as agreements, statutes and regulations. But Maybelle thinks of the transaction in terms of results. For example, although Delaware's General Corporation Law says that stockholders must adopt or reject the merger *agreement,* investors like Maybelle think of approving or rejecting a proposed *merger.*

In a merger proxy, it's important to summarize the conditions to the merger. The legal reflex is to repeat the conditions listed in the merger agreement. Many of these conditions are irrelevant to Maybelle, however, because they are extremely unlikely to happen. (Example: The NYSE refuses to list additional shares of an issue already listed.) Maybelle's list of conditions should only deal with live probabilities, and you probably shouldn't call them "conditions." That's legalese. They're "events" or "circumstances" that will prevent the merger.

Precision isn't everything. As lawyers, we might introduce a key player as "Prince Charming, Inc., a Delaware corporation ('Charming')." For sensible folk like Maybelle, Charming's state of incorporation is seldom important, and they don't need a definition to know what to call it. You can introduce the company as "Prince Charming, Inc." and then refer to it as Charming without using a definition that is, for nonlawyers, pure clutter.

Again, as lawyers, we know the difference between a stock dividend and a stock split—in a stock dividend new shares are issued, which increases the corporation's stated capital; in a stock split, the shares are divided, with no increase in stated capital. Stated capital doesn't interest Maybelle or any other investor, however, and most people use "stock split" for both splits and dividends. So references to a three-for-two stock split will usually be clearer to Maybelle than references to a one-for-two stock dividend, even if the latter is (legally) more accurate. (Exception: A 5% stock dividend is easier to understand than a 21-for-20 "split.")

Be blunt! Securities lawyers, having a well-founded fear of litigation, tend to favor turns of phrase that drain off all hints of conflict. Note the language quoted under "Termination Fees" below, which describes in soporific majesty how much it could cost Beauty to leave Charming standing at the altar and run off with Beast Corp. There's no point to screaming "Sue me!," but there's also no point to pretending that the proposed merger couldn't result in a Beauty contest, especially since you will have to prominently disclose the break-up fee.

In the accompanying box, I've given a few before-and-after examples of how to change overly precise, document-oriented language to simpler, clearer Maybelle-oriented language. Just remember: Write from the *investor's* perspective.

(Some of my "before" examples are taken from the September 1996 Bell Atlantic/NYNEX merger proxy, perhaps the first plain-English merger proxy. My rewrites should not be taken as criticism of that document, from which I have learned and lifted much. We all owe a debt to the anonymous lawyers who made that first voyage of exploration, and I mean no disrespect in suggesting that we have now traveled farther on the seas on which they first adventured.)

Before	After
Conditions to the Merger The completion of the merger depends upon meeting a number of conditions, including the following: (a) the approval of the holders of a majority of the stock of Beauty; (b) there shall have been no law enacted or injunction entered which effectively prohibits the merger or which causes a material adverse effect on either of our companies . . .	**What Circumstances Might Prevent the Merger?** Either Beauty or Beast can withdraw from the merger if: • the merger is not approved by Beauty's stockholders • government or court action prevents or has a material adverse effect on the merger.

Termination Fees	**What Happens if Beauty Receives a Better Offer?**
The merger agreement generally requires Beauty to pay Beast a termination fee of $200 million if the merger agreement terminates under certain circumstances and Beauty has received an offer to enter into a significant transaction with a third party.	Beauty must pay Charming a termination fee of $200 million if Beauty withdraws from the merger to accept an acquisition offer it believes superior to the merger.
The State of Kansas	Kansas
The Office of the Insurance Commissioner of the State of Wisconsin	The Wisconsin insurance commissioner
The Board of Governors of the Federal Reserve System	The Federal Reserve Board
What Are the Tax Consequences to Stockholders of the Merger?	**How Will I be Taxed on the Merger?**
We encourage you to read the merger agreement as it is the legal document that governs the merger.	

PROSPECTUS AND INDENTURE

Some of my friends insist that you can't write a securities prospectus in plain English unless the underlying documents are in plain English. On this view, when a prospectus describes a corporate bond, it is describing a set of legal relationships that are embodied in a separate legal agreement—usually called an indenture—between the issuer and a trustee for the bond holders.

This leaves us with two descriptions of the bonds: one in the indenture and one in the prospectus. This duality wasn't a problem, however, until the plain-English rule came along. Before the plain-English rule, a prospectus drafter would simply incorporate vast tracts of the indenture into the prospectus.

That solution may no longer be viable. A note to the rule cautions us to avoid "complex information copied directly from legal documents without any clear and concise explanation of the provision(s)." Despite this, many prospectuses still incorporate goodly chunks of the indenture (slightly modified to remove unnecessarily long sentences, embedded lists or other indelicacies) without any explanation, concise or otherwise. The SEC has apparently acquiesced in the view that prospectus recitals of indenture provisions are "magic words" that investors expect to see recited *verbatim*. (I have similar expectations when I visit my dentist.)

However, even if you copy large chunks of the indenture word for word into the prospectus, you're not going to copy the whole thing. Inevitably, the description of the bonds in the indenture will differ from the description in the prospectus. What do you do about those differences? Most lawyers view the indenture as the key document. Accordingly, they tuck a sentence like the following into the prospectus:

> The following summary describes certain terms of the bonds and is qualified in its entirety by reference to the indenture.

Here's a charmingly in-your-face statement of the same thought:

> The following description is a summary of the material provisions of the indenture. We urge you to read the indenture because it, and not this description, define your rights as a holder of the bonds.

Really? I'm often the last to know anything, but did someone repeal the Securities Act when I wasn't looking? The primary source of the investor's rights is the *prospectus,* not the indenture. How do I know? The Securities Act tells me so.[53]

Actually, there is no one source for all of the investor's rights. These rights arise from many sources, including the bankruptcy laws and the laws governing fiduciaries, and, of course, the securities laws. What, for example, is the source of the rights of holders of General Motors' common stock? GM's certificate of incorporation? The Delaware General Corporation Law? The Top 40 decisions of the Delaware Court of Chancery? Does it matter?

The prospectus and the indenture are each important, although partial, sources of the bond holders' rights. Most of the other sources aren't discussed in the prospectus because they aren't unique to the securities being issued. So the prospectus statement of rights is likely to have a good deal of overlap with the indenture because both describe those features of the bonds that distinguish them from other securities.

Still, there's no reason why the prospectus statement should be the same as the indenture statement. Because—stand back, I'm going to yell—*for investors, the description of the bonds in the indenture is the wrong description!* A prospectus, after all, should be written from the point of view of the *investor,* whereas an indenture is largely written from the point of view of the *trustee.*

A trustee is a plodding, serviceable sort of beast whose main interest is in doing what he's told without having to make any decisions. The indenture, in consequence, is largely a procedural document, not an economic one—on such-and-such dates, the trustee will transfer so-many-dollars to the paying agent's account number such-and-such. That sort of thing. (An indenture also deals with nonprocedural matters, such as covenants and default provisions, which should be described in the prospectus.)

There must be a tight relation between the indenture's description of the trustee's duties and the bond holders' economic interests. If the indenture does not give the proper instructions

53. *See, esp.*, sections 11 and 12.

to the trustee, the bond holders are not going to receive their 6%. Moreover, the trustee's disinclination to take any but ministerial actions assures that the processes for payment on the bonds and other matters will be described in mind-numbing detail. It's tempting to conclude that the more detailed description must be the more fundamental, but it's not always true. This is fortunate because it's easier to get a detailed step-by-step description wrong than a general description.

Suppose somebody made a mistake in drafting the indenture— if the indenture procedures are followed to the letter, the bond holders will not always receive their full interest. Would anyone argue that the bond holders are not entitled to the interest because of the drafting error? Of course not.

Most indentures contain provisions that allow the indenture to be amended to correct errors without bond holder consent. If the indenture were the fundamental source of the bond holders' rights, however, there *couldn't be* any errors. To allow for errors is to admit that other sources can override the indenture.

OK, so the traditional statement that "the following description is subject to the indenture" is out of bounds. What can you say, then, about the relation of the indenture to the prospectus?

In prospectuses my company has used for asset-backed securities, we tried to describe the securities as far as possible without reference to the underlying document. (In the asset-backed biz, the agreement between the issuer and the trustee is called a pooling and servicing agreement, or P&S.) We do, of course, have a section on the P&S that covers matters, such as amendments, for which reference to the P&S is unavoidable. The lead in to that section advises readers that:

> The securities are complex instruments, and the P&S is a lengthy and complex document. This prospectus only discusses those aspects of the securities and the P&S that we believe are likely to be material to you. You should read the P&S for provisions that are important to you. The trustee will send a copy of the P&S to you on your written request.

There are aspects of this warning that I find unsatisfying. For one thing, saying the P&S is a complex document is something of an understatement. Before plain English, the standard asset-backed prospectus was nearly impenetrable to anyone who didn't already know what it was supposed to say. But next to the P&S, that prospectus read like *Pat the Bunny*.

So cautioning an investor to read the P&S before investing might seem about as helpful as advising her to get an MBA. However, asset-backed securities are typically sold to a small number of institutional investors. (My company generally prints only 500 prospectuses per issuance.) A statement that would be ridiculous in a prospectus for a general audience—"read the P&S," for example—might be a useful warning in a prospectus for sophisticates, except that sophisticates already know to read the P&S. A more forthright (and useful) warning might go something like:

> "For sophisticated investors only! Don't buy unless you have a lot of money and an MBA on call!"

The SEC's official position, however, seems to be that a prospectus cannot assume sophisticated investors. The plain-English rule states that a prospectus must not contain any "legal jargon or highly technical business terms." Still, the Commission in practice seems to realize that what's highly technical in an IPO or a merger proxy might not be highly technical in an asset-backed securities prospectus. At least I hope so. I still flog the P&S in my prospectuses for asset-backed securities. On the other hand, whenever they let me near a merger proxy, I try to delete any injunctions to read the merger agreement. One of these days I'll get away with it.

SHELF REGISTRATION

A shelf registration prospectus consists of two parts, commonly labeled the *prospectus* and the *prospectus supplement*. The prospectus gives general background information about the issuer and the securities. It is preceded by the supplement, which describes the particular securities being issued—the amount, interest rate, maturity, underwriters, etc.

Suppose you register $10 billion of bonds. You can then issue $1 billion in January with a 5% interest rate and a 10-year maturity and another $800 million in February with a 15-year maturity and a 6% coupon. The prospectuses for the two issuances will be identical, but the supplements will vary to take account of the different terms of the bonds.

Breaking the document in two has produced confusion about the relation of the pieces. To begin with, the prospectus/supplement terminology does not square with the Securities Act or the rules. "Prospectus" is a statutory term that refers to the entire document consisting of the prospectus supplement and the so-called prospectus, which I'll now call the "core prospectus."

I suspect that the misuse of "prospectus" goes back to the early days of shelf registration. In by-gone times, registrants filed only the core prospectus with the registration statement. This made sense because a form of supplement would be a slender document consisting almost entirely of blanks. Consequently, calling the only thing that was filed the "prospectus" must have seemed unavoidable.

If your registration statement contains only a core prospectus, it makes sense to give the cover page of the core the full treatment the rules require for the cover page of a prospectus. This may explain why today the "cover" of a core prospectus, 44 pages deep in a prospectus, will sport the legends and other rigmarole that regulation s-k prescribes for a cover page.

The sec no longer lets you file a core prospectus without a prospectus supplement, and for good reason. Evolution in the securities markets has produced all sorts of securities whose specific terms can't be described in less than several dozen pages. There is no way an sec reviewer can understand these securities without seeing at least a mock-up of the prospectus supplement.

In prospectuses I recently worked on, we tried to clarify the relation of the core and the supplement right at the beginning: Immediately before or after the table of contents, we have a "How to read this prospectus" section, which explains that:

- the prospectus consists of a prospectus supplement followed by a core prospectus;
- the core gives general background information, whereas the supplement gives specific information about the securities being offered and
- the supplement may modify the information in the core. (This enabled us to drop most of the "Except as otherwise stated in the prospectus supplement . . ." language that normally runs wild throughout the core prospectus.)

We also dropped most of the statements in the core that such-and-such "will be explained in the applicable supplement." What is an investor to make of such a statement? For investors, there's only one supplement—the one they're holding in their hands—and they don't have to wait for it.

Most of this language comes from an understandable tendency of prospectus drafters to adopt the perspective of the SEC reviewer rather than the perspective of the investor. (Self-preservation, said Thomas Hobbes, is the first law of nature.) From the reviewer's perspective, a core prospectus is a document that will (future tense) be attached to many different supplements. From the investor's perspective, however, the core prospectus is presently firmly attached to one and only one prospectus supplement.

An investor, for example, does not have to be told in the core prospectus that the securities will be offered in a firm underwriting *or* a best efforts underwriting *or* a private placement. The prospectus supplement describes the particular mode of distribution; the various ways in which the securities are *not* distributed are of no interest to the investor. For the investor, it's clutter, but you can understand why an SEC reviewer would want to see it.

A core prospectus isn't expected to change with every issuance (or "takedown," as I'm learning to say), so there's a premium on having one-size-fits-all sections. These sections, however, are likely to contain lots of material that is of no value to an investor in the particular series described in the supplement.

My mortgage-backed securities core prospectus, for example, has a long section describing the legal difficulties in foreclosing on a mortgage loan, enforcing a due-on-sale clause or otherwise attempting to exercise contractual remedies in the seven states where most of our mortgaged properties are located. OK, said I, why don't we take the discussion of the individual state's laws out of the core. In any issuance, we can include in the supplement a discussion of only those states where there are a material number of mortgages.

"Great idea, kid!" said everyone, "but . . . no one is going to want to play around with the supplement at the last minute." Least of all, I had to admit, me. So our prospectus for securities backed solely by California mortgages still contains pages of information about how you foreclose a mortgage in the Nutmeg State, the Sunshine State, the Empire State, the Garden State, the Chicago State and the Great State of Texas.

We did, however, manage to place seven pages of information on adjustable rate mortgages (ARMs in the biz), buydown loans and agency certificates—stuff that we're unlikely to securitize—in an appendix. The core states that "if a series does not contain a material amount of ARMs, buydown loans or agency certificates, the appendix may be omitted." We've omitted it ever since. It'll be there in the unlikely event that we need it, and it's not there when it's not needed.

Cost and timing considerations may explain another oddity. The supplement invariably has its own page numbering system (S-1 to S-whatever). It would be more convenient for the reader to have a uniform numbering system for the whole prospectus but that would require rejiggering the core's pagination for each takedown of securities.

The core invariably carries its own date, which can be earlier than the supplement's date. This provides a succinct explanation of why the supplement can conflict with and override an earlier core but should provide little additional comfort. If the core is correct as of its date but materially incorrect at the date of the prospectus, you'd better make sure the supplement supplies the correction. If there's been a major development, cautious practitioners will want to revise the core. In our most recent prospectuses, we've abandoned separate dating for the core and the supplement; the sole date is on the front cover, and it's the date for the entire prospectus.

Prospectuses contain lots of defined terms. It's common for the core and the supplement to each contain its own index of defined terms. That's inconvenient because the normal expectation is that an index will be at the end. Moreover, it's hard to find the supplement's index, which is at the end of the supplement— that is, in the middle of the document. The obvious solution is to have a single index of defined terms at the end of the document just as you (now) have a single table of contents at the front.

At the very least you should have a table of contents at the front. Section 502 of regulation s-k says that you must ". . . on either the inside front or outside back cover page of the prospectus, provide a reasonably detailed table of contents." Nonetheless, I still see shelf registration prospectuses where the table of contents at the front is only for the supplement; deep in the document there's another table of contents for the core. I think this practice also goes back to the days when only the core was filed with the registration statement, but I can't see how splitting the table of contents in this way complies with today's rules. On the other hand, plain English is also a rule, and I still see many prospectuses that are a long way from compliance.

SUPPORTING PLAYERS

The agreement forms the core of the deal. Around the periphery of the agreement, however, hover other documents on which lawyers seldom focus, perhaps because they are so familiar. In this chapter, I review the performance of three familiar supporting players—amendments, promissory notes and guaranties.

AMENDMENTS

Some amendments are good, like the Bill of Rights, whereas some are bad, like Prohibition. The document amendments that lawyers draft are mainly inscrutable. Consider the following section of an amendment to a revolving credit agreement done in the standard manner:

> Section 5.2(b) is amended by substituting the amount "$10,000,000" for the amount "$5,000,000" in clause (vi) thereof.

Five million dollars of something is being done to someone, but you'd be hard-pressed to say what. The drafter (me, before I got religion) wrote the amendment as a set of instructions for a typist. You can't understand the amendment without pulling down the original agreement, finding the section and marking it up. A necessary exercise for lawyers but not something to be inflicted on civilians.

Here's a better way to write the same section:

> **Increase in debt basket.** Section 5.2, "Negative Covenants," p55, is amended to read as follows:

151

So long as the note remains unpaid or any lender has a commitment under this agreement, the borrower will not, nor will it permit any subsidiary to . . .

***

(b) **Debt.** have any debt, except debt . . . (vi) not otherwise permitted by this subsection (b) in an aggregate amount not to exceed ~~$5,000,000~~ <u>$10,000,000</u>. . . .

Among the revised amendment's various devices, the most obvious is the "blackline" style, with enough context included to show the nature of the change. That's right—the underlines and strikeouts are part of the final amendment. The amendment will, of course, have to explain early on that, where a textual passage is amended in part only, new language will be shown <u>double underlined</u>, deleted language will be shown in ~~strikeout~~, and language that is unmodified will be shown as an ellipsis (". . ."). The amendment should also provide that double underlining, deleted language and ellipses are for convenience only and not part of the agreement as amended.

There are some other improvements. The amendment section is titled informatively, the section to be amended is referenced by name as well as section number, and a page reference is given for readers who wish to consult the original.

Not every amendment can be made clear by blacklining, however. Consider the following:

Clause (b) of section 3.2 is amended to read as follows:

the representations and warranties contained in section 4 (other than those contained in subsections <u>(e),</u> (f) and (g)) are correct in all material respects as though made on and as of such date.

Blacklining clearly doesn't prove informative here. We can, however, make the amendment's effect clear by inserting a comment, such as:

The amendment eliminates as a condition to borrowing the representation in section 4(e) that "Since December 31,

2001, there has been no material adverse change in the ability of the borrower to perform its obligations under the agreement."

Comments, like examples, are explanatory devices that lawyers use too little.[54]

Amendments are usually organized to track the order of the original agreement. That is, amendments to section 2 usually come before amendments to section 3 and so forth. This is generally sensible, but departures are occasionally desirable. In particular, if a definition is added or modified solely to accommodate an amendment to another section, the new or modified definition should immediately precede (or follow) the section of the amendment in which it figures.

Amendments can create a lot of clutter. Someone raises a question about a provision of an agreement, so you take the agreement off the shelf. You also take down five other documents, namely, amendments one through five. Few things are more frustrating than trying to juggle a half-dozen documents so that you can interpret a section.

It would be nice if each time you amended an agreement, you produced an amended and restated version. But that can be expensive. In my own practice as in-house counsel, I frequently draft amendments to agreements that were originally created and are still controlled by outside counsel. I try to avoid paying outside counsel for an amendment and restatement. The solution I have adopted is to draft each amendment as a *cumulative* amendment. It's really quite simple: The amendment contains all the material in the preceding amendment and then provides that:

Except to the extent restated in this amendment, the provisions of the [preceding amendments] shall be of no further effect.

It's like the cumulative supplement to a lawbook. When a cumulative amendment becomes effective, I toss out the earlier amendments.

54. *See* "Explaining with Examples" beginning at 115.

Incidentally, in a cumulative amendment I use double under-lining and strikeout only to show changes from the preceding amendment. That way readers can identify those changes made by the latest cumulative amendment.

PROMISSORY NOTES

My affection for promissory notes resembles the affection that archaeologists feel for King Tut's tomb—the joy of encountering an abundance of antiquities in a small space. In the accompanying box entitled *Memorial Promissory Note* I've excerpted some illustrative promissory note language—by no means the worst of the genre—highlighting those passages that may provide particular delight to connoisseurs of the prolix.

Memorial Promissory Note

For value received, the undersigned Borrower Corp., a Delaware corporation, **hereby** promises to pay to **the order of** Lender Corp. at First National Bank, New York, NY on April 1, 2004 **in lawful money of the United States of America,** the principal sum of **ten million dollars ($10,000,000), with** interest **on the unpaid principal balance from the date hereof until maturity.**

Interest on this note shall accrue on any unpaid principal balance for each day during the term of this note at a per annum rate of 7%. Interest shall be computed on the basis of a year of 360 days and actual days elapsed. **Payment of interest** on the unpaid balance hereof **shall be made** in arrears on the first business day of each month **during the term hereof** and at maturity. **All payments of principal and interest shall be made** without setoff, deduction or counter-claim.

The Borrower **hereby** waives **diligence,** presentment, **demand, protest, notice of dishonor and notice of any kind whatsoever.**

In this section, I'll discuss those promissory notes I call *memorial* notes. These notes are used solely to evidence an obligation. They may be contrasted with what I call *commercial* notes, which are meant to be passed from holder to holder in the stream of commerce.

On the bookcase behind my desk entombed in Lucite rests in honored glory a commercial promissory note. It reads in its entirety (without signatures, countersignatures or corporate logo) as follows:

PROMISSORY NOTE
NOTE NUMBER 0000201   5/28/93 $8,248,000.00
On 6/01/93, for value received, SMITH BARNEY, HARRIS UPHAM & CO. INCORPORATED
Promises To Pay To The Order Of **BEARER**
The Sum Of $***8,248,000.00* PLUS INTEREST $*****2,676.89*** DOLLARS
Payable At Morgan Guaranty Trust Company of NY—New York, New York.

Things don't happen much faster than that.

Every year my employer issues billions of dollars of these notes (commonly referred to as *commercial paper*), a tiny fraction of the commercial paper in circulation. Few lawyers labor over the wording of commercial notes. No lender asks for more words nor would pay a fraction of a basis point for them. Contrary to the presupposition of most lawyers, lenders often prefer to rely on market practices unsullied by legalisms. No one wants to sit down and read fine print in commercial paper.

If you find it hard to believe that so much money can change hands with so little verbiage, reflect on the simplicity of another commercial instrument whose importance dwarfs that of the commercial note. I refer, of course, to the check. You give them, you take them, you seldom question their wording. The check collection system would not be improved by allowing clever people to modify the check's minimalist phraseology.

We may now proceed to nibble at the overstuffed prose of the memorial note, pausing for a few legal lessons along the way.

For value received. As luck would have it, the first words of the note raise interesting issues. First, despite the ubiquity of those three words (they even appear in my commercial note), the words are not necessary for an instrument to be a promissory note. Nothing in Article 3, "Negotiable Instruments," of the Uniform Commercial Code requires the phrase. (Article 3 comes in two flavors: 1952 (Article 3 *Classic*) and the 1990 revision. The 1990 revision has been adopted in most states, but there are some important holdouts, such as New York and Guam. Unless noted, everything said here applies to both versions.)

Article 3 will govern if the note is *negotiable*. This is not the place, nor am I the man, to initiate you into all the mysteries of negotiability. For the present, you need only understand that if a note meets the formal standards for negotiability set out in Article 3, certain holders of the note will not be subject to defenses of the maker of the note (i.e., the guy who signed it) or any prior endorser that would be available on a simple contract. Such a fortunate holder is called a *holder in due course.*

A holder in due course has to take the note for value and without notice of any defenses. A note's bare recital that it has been issued "for value received" is not much help in establishing holder in due course status. If you take a note from someone other than the maker, the maker's receipt of value doesn't establish that you gave value to the intermediary holder. If, however, you took the note directly from the maker, you are likely to have notice of any defenses.

Although "for value received" is unlikely to help establish holder in due course status, might it not be useful to a holder who is not a holder in due course? (There's no established terminology for a holder who is not a holder in due course; I'll call the unlucky fellow a *vulnerable holder*). Against a vulnerable holder, failure of consideration can be a defense, so having the note say that it is issued "for value received" may provide some evidence of consideration. For the typical commercial note, with its stripped-down wording, "for value received" might seem to have some (slight) evidentiary value.

As it happens, however, the maker or endorser of a negotiable promissory note has the burden under the UCC of establishing the defense of lack of consideration.[55] Even before the UCC, the courts had universally come to regard a negotiable note as carrying a presumption of consideration. This presumption

---

55. U.C.C. § 3-307(2) (1952); § 3-308(b) (1990).

became part of the Uniform Negotiable Instruments Law, the precursor to UCC Article 3.

In 19th century England, there were statutes—repealed more than a century ago—that required a note to recite "for value received" if interest and damages were to be recovered or if issued in payment for coal(!). In the middle of that century, some English authorities deemed it advisable to always insert "for value received" in a note, but that view seems to have died out well before the end of the century.[56]

Of course, many memorial notes do not need "for value received" to demonstrate consideration. For example, master or grid promissory notes describe the making of loans to the extent that "for value received" becomes superfluous. Other notes may refer to loan agreements or other documents that demonstrate consideration.

Even if your particular note doesn't on its face or by reference evidence consideration, how much should you worry? After all, failure of consideration is also a defense against a *check* held by a vulnerable holder. (By 1785, the English courts had settled that the words "for value received" were not necessary for bills of exchange, a category that includes checks.[57]) Yet few lawyers would decorate a check's memo line with "for value received." My guess is that, in the vast majority of cases, proving consideration will be quite easy without help from "for value received."

I have probably beaten this horse to death. Leaving in "for value received" does not make a note less readable. In addition, someone will add, the phrase might provide a bit of protection for a vulnerable holder. So why not leave the established practice alone?

If you're going to stay up nights worrying about lack of consideration, by all means leave in "for value received." The lesson comes from reflecting on how those six syllables got there. They arrived centuries ago for reasons I have not inquired into. They

---

56. I am indebted to Professor Bruce A. Campbell for acquainting me with some of the curious history of "for value received."

57. James Steven Rogers, The Early History of the Law of Bills and Notes 214 (1995).

have remained ever since because no one has had the will to remove them. The trembling associate doesn't know why the words are there but appreciates that no one will criticize their presence if they stay.

There is a slight probability that it might be handy some day to have "for value received" in our note. However, the only reason we insist on addressing this particular low probability is *because the words are already there.* We don't insist on adding these words to checks, and we don't (I hope) insist on adding clauses to our documents to address situations of similar low probability.

The argument against "for value received" is not that the words serve no conceivable use but that everything in a document should be directed toward outcomes whose expected value—the probability of the outcome multiplied by its cost—crosses some threshold. For example, if a 1% likely outcome would cost $10 billion, the expected value of the outcome is $100 million—enough to require our attention. If, however, the outcome would cost $1 million but is 0.01% likely, or is 1% likely but would cost only $10,000, the expected value is $100—not worth legal time and resources.

We seldom know the exact probability of an outcome and often can't compute its exact cost. We should, however, develop a gut feel for probability and cost that is a good enough basis to judge the utility of a provision. A recurrent theme in these pages is that lawyers should have more guts.

We may now turn to the other highlighted language in the memorial promissory note.

"The undersigned." You'll want to spell out the name of the maker so that you can add identifiers such as "a Delaware corporation." "The undersigned" is therefore redundant, besides being a bit stiff.

"Hereby." The sentence begins "[maker] promises to pay . . .," not "[maker] promised to pay," "[maker] will promise to pay" or "[maker] would promise to pay." There are times we have to distinguish an action taken by the document from an action merely referred to. This is not one of those times.[58]

---

58. *See* "Words—Hereof, Thereof and Everywhereof" at 5.

The order of. If a note is payable "to" someone rather than payable "to the order of" someone, the note will not be negotiable. For memorial notes (as opposed to commercial paper and similar notes that are intended to be passed around), however, negotiability may be impossible or undesirable. I frequently draft promissory notes between subsidiaries, primarily for the comfort of our auditors. These notes display an annoying tendency to get themselves lost. I therefore leave out "to the order of" and title these notes "non-negotiable promissory note." It helps me sleep at night.

If you want your note to be negotiable, you'll need "to the order of." Just be careful what you want.

"In lawful money of the United States of America." The legal pen at work. In a note between a domestic maker and a domestic payee that is governed by the law of one of these United States, won't "$" do the trick? If the note truly has some transnational aspect, "US$" will work. (Have you ever seen a check drawn on a US bank indicate the provenance of the currency by anything more than "$"?)

"Ten million dollars ($10,000,000)." This would best be replaced by "$10 million." Note that the pros—the people who fill in the blanks in commercial paper—use numerals alone rather than words alone or numerals and words together. My appeal to authority is not totally convincing here, however, because the pros would also write the number as "$10,000,000.00." In my view, writing all those zeros, plus the useless recitation of cents, is asking for trouble.[59]

"On the unpaid balance, etc." This clause says nothing that isn't said in the first sentence of the following paragraph.

"Payment of interest shall be made." A few extra words give it that artistic touch. Try "interest shall be paid" or (even better) "[maker] shall pay interest. . . ."

Diligence, demand, protest, notice of dishonor. The 1952 version of Article 3 provides that "where without excuse any necessary presentment or notice of dishonor is delayed beyond the

---

59. For the reasoning behind my views, *see* "Words—Words and Numbers" at 7.

time when it is due . . . any [e]ndorser is discharged. . . ." Presentment (for our purposes, a demand upon the maker for payment) must be made on the date the note is due. Moreover, if the maker refuses to pay (i.e., dishonors) the note, the holder has to give an endorser notice of the dishonor before midnight of the third business day following dishonor. So if a note endorsed to you matures on April 1, 2004, you had better present the note for payment on April 1 and, if it is dishonored, notify the endorser within three days. Or have a good excuse. Or a waiver.[60]

The rule dates from at least 1703. "In the late seventeenth century and throughout the eighteenth century . . . the issue of what was a reasonable time for presentment seems to have accounted for a fairly large percentage of . . . bills and notes cases. . . ."[61]

1990 Article 3 is more relaxed. An endorser is only discharged if the holder fails to give notice of dishonor within 30 days of dishonor. For a note payable on a fixed date, dishonor occurs automatically (i.e., without presentment) on that date if the note is not paid.[62]

Waiving presentment and notice of dishonor is, therefore, potentially important, and it only takes four words. Article 3 (1990) says that waiving presentment also waives notice of dishonor. Under the 1952 version, waiver of protest waives presentment and notice of dishonor. So "The borrower waives presentment" (or "waives protest" under 1952 Article 3) does the trick.[63]

This is true at least for negotiable notes. What about non-negotiable notes? The comments to Article 3 (1990) says that ". . . it may be appropriate . . . for a court to apply one or more provisions of Article 3 to [an instrument that is not negotiable] by analogy . . . ,"[64] Thus, a waiver that works for negotiable instruments is likely to work for non-negotiable instruments.

60. U.C.C. §§ 3-502(1), 3-504(1), 3-508(2) (1952).
61. ROGERS, *supra* note 56, at 202–204.
62. U.C.C. §§ 3-503(c), 3-502(a)(3) (1990).
63. U.C.C. § 3-505(b) (1990); § 3-511(5) (1952).
64. U.C.C. § 3-104, cmt. 2 (1990).

Incidentally, our commercial note doesn't need a waiver of presentment or protest. Because it is payable to bearer, it is negotiated by delivery. The liability of endorsers is therefore usually irrelevant.

Do today's longer-winded notes give added protection?

"The notes used to be so square," he said, holding a pair of index fingers six inches apart. "'I promise to pay.'" Now, said Carter, indicating a telephone directory, the documents are "so thick." He said that the shorter ones were harder to get out of. "There is no defense for 'I promise to pay,'" he said.[65]

GUARANTIES

Nobody loves you when you're down and out, unless, of course, you have your parent's guaranty. It's a simple idea: The Worrywart Whistle Works (*On the Web at www.wwww.com!*) won't supply whistles to thinly-capitalized Junior Corp. unless Daddy Corp. guarantees Junior's obligations. Daddy is to have much the same obligations on the guaranty as Junior has on the whistle supply agreement.

Sad to say, this simple idea often results in a complicated document with some potentially nasty surprises.

Paraphrasing the 1996 Restatement of the Law (Third) of Suretyship and Guaranty (§ 1), Daddy will be a guarantor of Junior's obligations to Worrywart if, pursuant to contract, Worrywart has recourse against Daddy for Junior's obligations to Worrywart. (Some other things also have to be true for Daddy to be a guarantor, but this is enough for now.)

The first thing to notice about guaranties is that Daddy becomes a guarantor "pursuant to contract." The contract in questions is the guaranty or, to put the proper spin on it, *a guaranty is a contract!* Accordingly, Daddy and Worrywart can sculpt the guaranty to do whatever they mutually desire. The law of guaranty is thus partly a set of default rules—what you get unless you agree to something else.

65. JAMES GRANT, MONEY OF THE MIND (1992).

A guaranty is more than a contract, however, for it involves three separate relationships, one of which is usually not contractual: First (using the Restatement's lingo), Junior has an *underlying obligation* to Worrywart to pay for the whistles. Second, Daddy has a *secondary obligation,* embodied in the guaranty, to pay Worrywart for the whistles if Junior doesn't. Third, Junior will have reimbursement and other obligations to Daddy if Daddy pays Worrywart under the guaranty. Junior's obligations to Daddy (No, they're not called "tertiary obligations") could be modified by agreement, but seldom are. (For unrelated parties, these obligations are often covered by indemnity agreements. Restatement §18.)

For each of these obligations, there are reciprocal obligations of the other party, and (here the problems begin) a party may have defenses based on the conduct of the other two players. Most importantly, Daddy could be partially or totally discharged from its guaranty if Worrywart takes certain actions that increase Daddy's risk, such as releasing Junior or Junior's collateral from the underlying obligation.

The trickiest task in most guaranties is to allow the guarantor the proper defenses. As a guarantor, Daddy will generally have two sorts of defenses against Worrywart. First, Daddy will have what I shall call the "Junior defenses"—all those defenses that Junior has against Worrywart under the whistle supply agreement, except for discharge in bankruptcy and lack of capacity (Restatement §34). If, for example, Junior is not liable to pay because Worrywart delivered wheezy whistles, Daddy should not be liable on the guaranty.

Little need be said about the bankruptcy exception to the Junior defenses, but "capacity" requires a closer look. When does a corporation lack "capacity"? The Restatement includes in lack of capacity a corporation's entering into a contract that is beyond its powers (§ 34, illustration 7). But suppose Junior has the power to contract for whistles, but did not duly authorize the contract? Because of the relationship between Daddy and Junior, it seems inequitable to allow Daddy to escape liability because Junior has a defense of lack of authorization. After all, Daddy knew enough about the supply agreement to sign the guaranty. Worrywart may therefore want Daddy to waive all defenses based on Junior's failure to authorize the agreement.

Besides any Junior defenses, Daddy may also have defenses that arise directly out of Daddy's status as a guarantor—the *suretyship defenses*. ("Suretyship" is the legal domain of which the law of guaranty forms one of the larger precincts.)

Suretyship law long predates subsidiary corporations. (*The Merchant of Venice,* my favorite commercial law play, revolves around a suretyship obligation.) In the non-corporate world, a guarantor might be a relative or other person who can not control the parties to the underlying transaction. The law of guaranty sensibly protects the guarantor against the other parties' deliberately or inadvertently increasing the guarantor's risk. Such conduct will often provide a guarantor with a complete or partial defense to a claim under the guaranty. (Guaranties tend to be read in favor of the guarantor; see, e.g., Portia's reading of Antonio's bond, *In re Shylock,* 43 Bard.App.3d 471(*ca* 1598)).

The various suretyship defenses make little sense, however, when a company guarantees its subsidiary's obligations. Daddy Corp. is likely to have firm control over Junior Corp. Moreover, any benefit that Worrywart grants to Junior is likely to benefit Daddy as well. (Section 48(2) of the Restatement addresses this situation in part by providing that consent by a subsidiary to an act that would otherwise give its parent a suretyship defense will generally constitute consent to that act by the parent.)

Since a guaranty is a contract, Worrywart may properly insist that Daddy waive the suretyship defenses. Unfortunately, the law of suretyship is largely judge-made, with no authoritatively complete list of the suretyship defenses. Worrywart may respond to this uncertainty by having Daddy disclaim a laundry list of specific defenses. This often takes several pages, and at the end Worrywart may still fear that a defense has been missed. Accordingly, Worrywart may buttress the specific waivers with a general waiver of "all other defenses."

Call me paranoid, but this last scares me. Mightn't a waiver of "all other defenses" waive the Junior defenses as well as the suretyship defenses? The context may argue against it, and I don't believe that "all defenses" has to mean *all* defenses, but I'd hate to learn the contrary the hard way. After all, (Greek chorus) "a guaranty is a contract," so a court could hold that Daddy agreed to waive some or all of the Junior defenses. How can Daddy make it clear that it is waiving the suretyship defenses but not the Junior defenses?

The Restatement favors a refreshingly direct path out of these perplexities: Daddy can waive all (and only) the suretyship defenses with the statement "Daddy Corp. waives all suretyship defenses." That's all there is to it. (§ 48(1) and illustration 3).

Will the Restatement's formula for waiving suretyship defenses be effective in your jurisdiction? A restatement is not the law, only a codification of the law by a respected bunch of legal eagles. It's persuasive, not precedential. Moreover, the Restatement is too new to have been cited approvingly by many courts.

If you're worried about your jurisdiction's acceptance of the Restatement's one sentence waiver, you can buttress it with a second sentence such as "The parties intend the preceding waiver of suretyship defenses to have the effects described in section 48 of the Restatement (Third) of the Law of Suretyship and Guaranty." The waiver thus drags in the Restatement, not as a statement of governing law but as a statement of the intent of the parties. Remember [here, trumpets], a guaranty is a contract![66]

Some guaranties say that "the guarantor's obligation under this guaranty is primary and not secondary." This is a flat out falsehood—if it's a primary obligation, then it can't be a guaranty! Nonetheless, such a statement may work as a waiver of suretyship defenses. The Restatement (§ 48, comment d) gently allows that:

> A statement to the effect that the secondary obligor does
> not have suretyship status, while inaccurate, is ordinarily

---

66. If you're still squeamish, you might try the marginally fatter waiver sanctified by § 3-605(i) of the 1990 version of Article 3 of the Uniform Commercial Code, which provides that an endorser of a negotiable instrument (who is a guarantor) can waive all suretyship defenses by stating that it "waives all defenses based on suretyship or impairment of collateral."

sufficient [to waive the suretyship defenses], however, because by communicating the absence of that status, it communicates that the incidents of suretyship status . . . are unavailable.

However, if you want to waive the suretyship defenses, there's no need to dabble in contradiction. Just say "Daddy waives all suretyship defenses."

Saying that Daddy's obligations are primary isn't correct, but it's not entirely wrong-headed. A primary obligor would have the Junior defenses but not the suretyship defenses. When the Worrywarts of this world insist that Daddy waive "all defenses," I often propose that we follow that waiver with a statement that "the parties intend that Daddy shall have only those defenses under this guaranty that Daddy would have if it were a co-obligor with Junior on the supply agreement."

Okay, let's get to the question you've really been itching to ask: How do you spell it? Is it "guaranty" or "guarantee"? The Restatement does not discuss spelling, but it uses "guaranty" for the noun throughout, with "guaranties" for the plural and "guarantee(s)" as the verb. In the Restatement, you draft a *guaranty* (or several *guaranties*, if business is good), but you *guarantee* an obligation.

Bryan Garner's *Dictionary of Modern Legal Usage* states that the old distinction in British English between the noun form *guaranty* and the verb form *guarantee* has broken down both here and in Great Britain. Today:

> [the noun] *guarantee* is the usual term, seen often, for example, in the context of consumer warranties or other assurances of quality or performance. *Guaranty,* in contrast, is now used primarily in financial and banking contexts in the sense of "a promise to answer for the debt of another." *Guaranty* is now rarely seen in nonlegal writing, whether in Great Britain or in the United States.

"Guaranty" may be the rarer bird these days, but it has the more precise legal sense that we are concerned with and should be preferred.

Now we can start drafting. Your first sentence should read something like "Daddy Corp. guarantees to the Worrywart Whistle Works the obligations of Daddy's subsidiary, Junior Corp., under the supply agreement dated April 1, 2002 between Junior and Worrywart." Nifty. Mentioning that Junior is Daddy's subsidiary isn't necessary, but may help a reader understand the business and legal context.

Standard guaranties frequently expand this sentence to say something like "Daddy *absolutely and unconditionally* guarantees . . ." (Sometimes they add *irrevocably,* which I'll get to in a bit.) What do the extra words contribute?

I've seen "absolutely and unconditionally" used in front of "indemnifies," "promises to pay" and a number of other verbs. Garner doesn't have an entry for either word, and Black's doesn't give the words any particular "legal" meaning. In most legal contexts, the words "absolutely and unconditionally" have no other function than to produce that tone of high solemnity deemed appropriate for a legal obligation. You can read them as synonymous with "Yea, verily."

But—surprise!—"absolutely and unconditionally" actually mean something (maybe a couple of things) when used in a guaranty, though I doubt you could tell me what. (If you think they might be adequate to waive suretyship defenses, forget it. They don't. Restatement § 48, comment d.)

An "absolute guaranty" is one that is effective without Worrywart's having to notify Daddy of its acceptance of the guaranty. Restatement § 8, comment a. This may be desirable, but I wouldn't want to do it with a word as mysterious as "absolute." Better just to say "This guaranty will be effective without notice of acceptance by Worrywart." No one is likely to be blindsided by that sentence.

In many jurisdictions, an "absolute" or "unconditional" guaranty also means a guaranty that can be enforced by Worrywart immediately upon Junior's default; Worrywart won't have to indulge in any niggling legal formalities, such as suing Junior, but can go straight to Daddy. This contrasts with a *guaranty of collection,* which Worrywart can only enforce against Daddy after an execution of judgment against Junior is returned unsatisfied, or if Junior is bankrupt, cannot be served or if it is otherwise apparent that payment cannot be obtained from Junior (Restatement 15(b)).

The Restatement doesn't have any nomenclature for an absolute (or unconditional) guaranty, probably because every guaranty is enforceable against the parent immediately upon default of the subsidiary unless the guaranty says otherwise. In many jurisdictions, however, such a guaranty is called a *guaranty of payment*. It's not necessary to state that a guaranty is a guaranty of payment, but if you want to hammer the point, don't say that the guaranty is "absolute and unconditional." Say "This guaranty is a guaranty of payment and not of collection." Phrases like "absolute and unconditional" are the bane of legal drafting—they generally mean nothing, except when they mean something unexpected.

A guaranty can, and often does, contemplate a continuing series of obligations. For example, the agreement between Worrywart and Junior may look forward to a whole series of whistle shipments and payments. A guaranty that covers these future obligations is called a *continuing* guaranty (Restatement §§ 15(e), 16). If the context doesn't make it clear, your guaranty should say "This guaranty is a continuing guaranty."

Under several legal theories (none of which need trouble us here), Daddy can terminate its guaranty of Junior's future obligations by notifying Worrywart (Restatement § 16). Worrywart can then decide if it wants to continue to deal with Junior on an unguaranteed basis. Daddy's termination will not, however, terminate its guaranty of any obligations Junior incurred prior to Daddy's notifying Worrywart of the termination.

Because Daddy's obligations under a continuing guaranty will only be terminable as to Junior's future obligations, you do not need to style your guaranty as "irrevocable." If the guaranty is continuing, calling it "irrevocable" might cut off Daddy's right to terminate its obligations as to Junior's future whistle purchases. This is seldom a good idea. It makes sense that Daddy may want to cut off its obligations under its guaranty, and the notice requirement means that Worrywart will not be caught unawares. (If the whistle supply agreement has been properly drafted, it will enable Worrywart to terminate if the guaranty is revoked.) The guaranty should, however, provide for a short period between Daddy's notice of termination and its effectiveness, so that Worrywart will have adequate time to react.

Guaranties often provide that Daddy's obligations will be reinstated if Worrywart has to return a payment made by Junior, as might happen if Junior's payment is held to be a voidable preference. A good thought, but hardly novel. Basic guaranty law requires reinstatement of the obligation under these circumstances (Restatement § 70), so there's no need to spell it out in the guaranty.

Guaranties frequently have dollar and time limits. For example, Daddy's liability under the guaranty might be capped at $1 million and limited to whistles ordered before October 31, 2005. There's no legal problem with including such limits in a guaranty. Whether you have such limits will depend on the transaction and the parties. A guaranty with such limits places a monitoring burden on Worrywart; without them, the monitoring burden is on Daddy. If the Worrywart-Junior transaction has dollar and time limits, Worrywart will already have the monitoring burden, so mirroring those limits in the guaranty makes sense.

If the underlying transaction does not have a dollar limit or a fixed termination date, it may make more sense to place the monitoring burden on Daddy. Generally, Daddy might be expected to know about Junior's activities. However, if Daddy's headquarters are many leagues removed from Junior's, and if Daddy has many other subsidiaries in diverse businesses, Daddy may monitor Junior less closely and may try to put some of the monitoring burden on Worrywart.

Under the law of guaranty, if Daddy pays a limited guaranty obligation in full, Daddy will, to the extent of its payment, be subrogated to Worrywart's claim against Junior. But if Daddy pursues its claim, it is likely to be competing against Worrywart. Accordingly, the guaranty may require Daddy to delay pursuing subrogation claims against Junior until Worrywart has been fully satisfied. Worrywart may also want Daddy to subordinate its other claims against Junior to Worrywart's claims. Whatever the equity of such provisions in a guaranty by an unrelated party, they seem fair enough in the context of a parent guaranty.

Finally, since (you probably saw this one coming) a guaranty is a contract, you will probably want some relevant contractual boilerplate. A choice of law section is usually desirable, as is a clause against oral amendments. Note that while the guaranty will likely only be signed by Daddy, you will usually want any amendments signed by both Daddy and Worrywart.

CONCLUSION

If you've gotten this far, you're probably itching to try some of the techniques I've described. Well, you've got your work cut out for you. For one thing, your efforts may not be appreciated, at least by other lawyers. Law is both relentlessly formal and relentlessly conservative—formal rebels are likely to be dealt with summarily. As I've said several times in these pages, it's going to take a little courage.

It's also going to take a lot of time, time you may not have. Most legal documents are produced by modifying documents written in the antique style I've railed against. Unfortunately, the pressures of transactional practice may deny you the time for the major make-over such documents deserve. But you can at least make a start. Make some changes now, and next time you can start where you left off. Eventually, you might accumulate a body of documents that go most of the way towards readability.

Just remember: You will understand the documents no matter how opaque they are. That's your job. The purpose of this book is to help you produce documents that Mork and Mindy Executive can understand. That, too, should become your job.

It's just common courtesy. In my office, there's a coffee station. The unwritten rule is that if you take the last cup, you make coffee for the next guy. That doesn't stop some people, who are no more pressed for time than everyone else these days, from walking off leaving two ounces in the pot. But that's not you. *You* are going to make sure your clients smell the coffee.

ABOUT THE AUTHOR

Howard Darmstadter has been practicing business law in New York City since 1977 and has been a lawyer for Citigroup Inc. and its predecessors since 1985.

Since 1993, Darmstadter has published three or four columns a year on legal documentation under the heading "Legal-Ease" in *Business Law Today,* the magazine of the American Bar Association's Section of Business Law. In 2000, Legal-Ease won the American Society of Business Publications Editors' national Gold Award for editorial excellence. Darmstadter has also published in *The Business Lawyer* and *The Uniform Commercial Code Law Journal.*

From 1966 to 1974, Darmstadter taught philosophy at the University of Wisconsin, New York University and the University of Massachusetts—Boston.

Darmstadter holds an A.B. from the University of Pennsylvania, a Ph.D. from Princeton University and a J.D from Harvard Law School. He lives in Stamford, Connecticut with his wife, Patricia Lydon, their sons, David and Michael Darmstadter Lydon, and two cats who prefer to remain anonymous.

INDEX